COLLINS GEM
ANTIQ
MARKS

G000125950

GEM
RD

COLLINS G
CRICKE

FAT

GEM
AID

COLLINS GEM
INTERNET
Connect
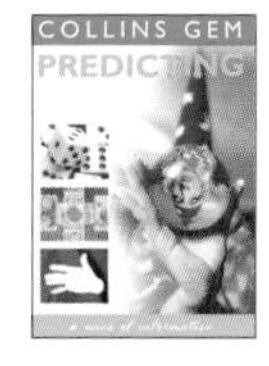
COLLINS GEM
PREDICTING

COLLINS GEM
Ready
REFERENCE

COLLINS GEM
SHARKS

COLLINS GEM
WHALES
& DOLPHINS

COLLINS GEM
WHISKY

COLLINS GEM
WORD
PROCESSING

COLLINS GEM
Your PC

COLLINS GEM

CHEESES

Jenny Linford

HarperCollins*Publishers*

Jenny Linford, the Teletext food and drink writer, regularly contributes to national newspapers and magazines. She has written several cookery books, including *Tastes of the Orient*, *Food Lovers' London* **and** *The Tate Gallery Restaurant*, **and she also conducts gastronomic tours of London.**

HarperCollins Publishers
Westerhill Road, Bishopbriggs, Glasgow G64 2QT

First published 2000

Reprint 10 9 8 7 6 5 4 3 2 1 0

Photographs by Christina Jansen

With thanks for all their help to: Patricia Michelson of La Fromagerie; Evan O'Riordan and David Lockwood of Neal's Yard; Robin Condon of Ticklemore Cheese; Cheeses, London N10; and Brindisa, London SE1.

ISBN 0 00 472375 9

Printed in Italy by Amadeus S.p.A.

Contents

Introduction

When one stops to think about it, it is astonishing that from one basic foodstuff – milk – should come such a diverse variety of cheeses: mellow, crumbly Parmesan; pungent blue-veined cheeses such as Stilton, Roquefort and Gorgonzola; smooth, creamy French Brie . . . the list goes on and on. Cheeses are a tangible, edible tribute to mankind's ingenuity.

In the age of a 'global village', when increasingly so many things are interchangeable from place to place, cheeses still reflect national, indeed regional characteristics, stemming as they do from specific locations and agricultural traditions. England's West Country, with its rich grassland and strong dairy heritage, is traditionally home to its best-known cheese, Cheddar. The great mountain cheeses of Switzerland and France such as Beaufort and Emmenthal are characterised by the floral, grassy aroma of the milk from which they are produced; milk from hardy mountain cattle grazed on alpine pastures. In Southern Italy, the rich milk of the water buffalo used to work the land was transformed into smooth, white mozzarella cheeses, delicious eaten with the local sweet tomatoes and a touch of olive oil.

A French sheep's cheese known as Coeur de Poiterin

THE HISTORY OF CHEESE

Cheese is an ancient food, thought to date back to around 9000 BC when milk-yielding animals were domesticated in Europe and the Middle East. Archaeologists have found references to cheese dating as far back as 4000 BC in a Sumerian cattle-breeder's records. These records tell us that the breeder's herd of cattle increased fivefold over eight years, with cheese production increasing eightfold over the same period. The first cheeses would have been made with goat's and sheep's milk, as the cow was the last dairy animal to be domesticated.

Curdling the milk

Given that the basic starting point of cheesemaking involves curdling the milk, it is tempting to speculate that cheese was first created by accident when milk left in hot sunshine soured and turned to curd. Once discovered, cheesemaking was a wonderful way to preserve valuable surplus milk and transform it into a high-protein food which could be stored for times when food was scarce. This is especially so in the early days of animal husbandry, when people had not yet discovered how to manipulate their livestock into producing milk year round. Throughout its history, cheese has been an important foodstuff in rural communities, especially in the days before railways and refrigeration allowed for the safe transporting of milk across considerable distances.

Shaping the cheese

Once curd cheese had been discovered the next step was to improve its texture by draining it. The Italian word for cheese, *formaggio*, and the French word, *fromage*, both come from the Latin word *forma*, meaning 'mould' or 'shape', and refer to the wicker baskets traditionally used to drain cheese.

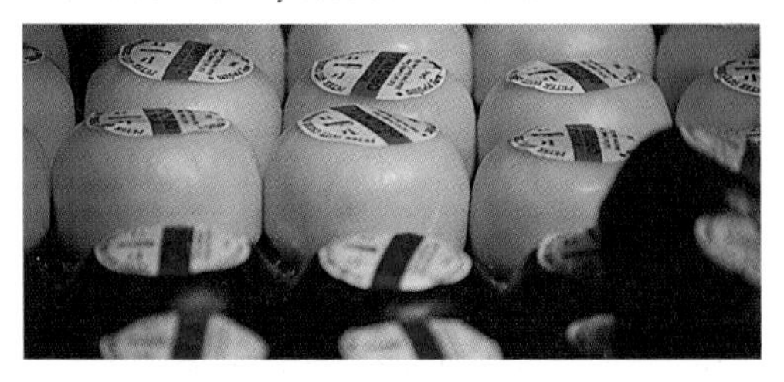

Every type of cheese has a traditional shape

The existence of hard cheese is thought to have come about before pottery came into general use. The shepherds and goatherds would have carried milk in containers made from the stomachs or bladders of slaughtered animals. The lining of a calf's stomach contains an enzyme, rennin, which produces rennet, a curdling agent. Therefore, milk kept in a calf's stomach bag would have coagulated and become firm.

Spreading cheesemaking skills

Cheese has long been valued as a protein-rich food. The ancient Greeks, who believed it was a gift from

Aristaeus, the son of the god Apollo, fed their Olympian athletes on a diet rich in this new product.

The Romans are known to have been cheese-eaters, with a special penchant for smoked cheese. Cheese was the perfect food for an army on the move, portable and filled with protein, so as the Roman Empire stretched across Europe so cheesemaking skills were passed to the people they colonised. In around AD 50 Columella, a former Roman soldier, wrote *De Re Rustica*, a manual aimed at soldiers leaving the army and planning to become farmers, which includes rules for the making of cheese. An even more tangible trace of the Romans' influence on cheesemaking is the fact that the English word 'dairy' comes from the Latin *dey*, meaning 'female servant', as the dairy has historically been a woman's domain.

Following the fall of the Roman Empire and the Dark Ages, it fell to religious orders to continue spreading cheesemaking skills. Monks are thought to have had a special interest in cheesemaking as it offered a way to vary their diet on fasting days, when meat was forbidden. French Cistercian monks brought to England by William the Conqueror in 1066 introduced cheesemaking skills to Yorkshire, where their great monasteries were based. Consequently there is a wide tradition of Dales cheeses dating back to that time.

Following the dissolution of the monasteries by Henry VIII in the 1530s, monks integrated with the community, often working on farms where they passed on the valuable skill of cheesemaking. In England there was a growth of 'territorial' cheeses, associated with a particular place. In Europe monasteries continued to thrive, hence cheesemaking was associated with monks for centuries. In France a certain type of washed-rind cheese, of which Port-Salut is a factory-made example, is still associated with Trappist monasteries where they were made. In Switzerland Tête-de-Moine is also a famous monastic cheese.

While cheese is made in many countries around the world, it is really only done so in those with a strong, long-standing dairy tradition. In the continents of Africa and most of Asia there is little tradition of cheesemaking: in fact, in China, Japan and Korea cheese is generally regarded with considerable suspicion. India, where the cow is sacred, is the only Asian country with a tradition of cheesemaking, and both cow and water buffalo milk is used.

MAKING CHEESE

The first step in cheesemaking is to curdle the milk. This is done by adding a 'starter culture' which causes the acid levels in the milk to rise, making the milk curdle. In the majority of cheeses, rennet is also added, causing the milk to separate into curds and whey.

The next stage is to separate the curds away from the liquid whey. Once this has been achieved, there are numerous factors which will affect the final cheese that is produced. The texture of the cheese is affected by how much whey is removed from the curds. Curds that are simply drained without being pressed retain more

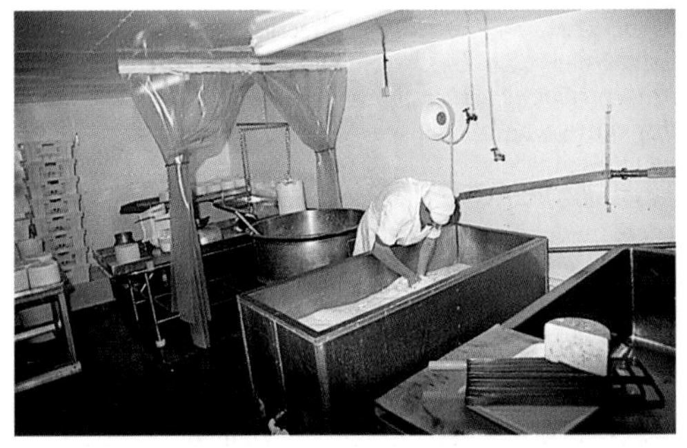

Checking the texture of the curds

moisture and result in a softer, moister cheese such as cream cheese. If pressure is applied to the cheese, then these 'pressed' cheeses become drier and can range in texture from 'semi-soft' through 'semi-hard' to 'hard'. Heating the curds can also affect the final texture.

Salting the cheese is an important part of preserving it. It is done in a number of different ways; some cheeses are soaked in brine (a salt solution), while others are rubbed with dry salt.

The careful encouragement of mould is used by cheesemakers making mould rind cheeses, such as Camembert, or blue-veined cheeses such as Roquefort. Ripening is the final stage in cheesemaking. Fresh soft cheeses will ripen within a few days or weeks. A hard cheese like a Cheddar will be ripened for many months. Different cheeses require different conditions of storage during ripening. Some need a warm, moist atmosphere to encourage the growth of certain beneficial bacteria, while others need a cool, well-ventilated atmosphere.

CHEESE TYPES

Although there are a bewildering variety of cheeses, they all fall into much broader categories of cheese types, depending upon how they are made.

The first point of distinction is the milk-type used: cow, goat, sheep or water buffalo. The differences in flavour between these milks will come through in the cheeses from which they are made.

Fresh cheeses

These are soft, moist, delicate cheeses without a rind or any mould. The simplest of these, known as lactic cheeses, are made by heating the milk and adding in a starter culture, but in many cases rennet is added which causes the milk to coagulate. To make soft fresh cheese the curd is wrapped in cloth or placed in perforated containers and drained without any pressure.

Whey cheeses

These are made by re-heating the whey from which the curds have been extracted: Italian ricotta cheese is a classic example. In Norway the whey is boiled down considerably to create a sweet, sticky, caramel-like cheese called Gjetost.

There are eight broad categories of cheese

STRETCHED CURD CHEESES

For these, heated curd is pulled or kneaded and then formed into balls or plaits. Italian Mozzarella cheese is a classic example.

BLOOMY MOULD RIND CHEESES

Curds are mixed with rennet, then drained, shaped and coated with a bacteria culture to encourage the growth of the desired bacteria. They are then left to ripen. A white bloomy rind is the characteristic of this group of cheeses, which includes two of France's best-known cheeses: Brie and Camembert.

Washed rind cheeses

Often rather pungent cheeses, these have a characteristic orange-brown sticky rind. As the name suggests, these are cheeses which are washed with brine, wine or marc brandy to encourage a particular orange bacteria and discourage mould. These bacteria work on the cheese from the skin. French Cabecou is an example.

Blue-veined cheeses

The curds are cut, sometimes stirred and cultured with bacteria during formation to give the characteristic blue-green veining through cheeses such as Stilton or Roquefort.

Pressed cheeses

The curd is mixed with rennet and the draining process is aided by cutting the cheese, stirring and pressing it to remove excess moisture. Classic examples include Cheddar, Edam, Pecorino and Saint-Nectaire.

Pressed and cooked cheeses

A similar process to the one above, but the curd is also heated during the cutting and stirring stages producing a characteristic

Pressed cheeses range in texture from semi-soft to hard

nutty flavour and smooth golden paste. Classic examples include Comte and Gruyère.

FRENCH CHEESES

The French are justifiably proud of their cheeses. No other country in the world produces such a huge variety, with around 500 different cheeses. Many of the world's great cheeses are French, such as Camembert or Roquefort.

One important way in which traditional French cheesemaking has been protected has been through a series of regulations known as Appellation d'Origine Controllée (AOC). These define specific cheeses, stipulating in which area of France they should be made and ensuring that key elements of the cheesemaking process are followed, ranging from the breed of cattle that provides the milk to the length of ripening time.

There are four types of cheese production permitted under AOC:

Fermier: made in a farmhouse, alpine chalet or mountain hut by an individual producer using his or her own unpasteurised milk.

Artisanal: made by an individual producer using milk from his or her farm or bought-in milk.

Co-operatives: made in a single dairy from milk provided by members of the co-operative.

Industrial: Industrially produced from milk bought from a number of producers.

Increasingly nowadays, despite the variety of cheeses to be found, factory-made versions of cheeses dominate the marketplace and handmade, farmhouse French cheeses are harder to find. The growth of supermarkets, which prefer to stock factory-made cheeses to fermier or artisanal ones, has been a powerful factor in this process. Handmade cheese requires skilful, knowledgeable handling to ensure that it matures successfully and careful tending to keep it in good condition. Fine cheese has been an area which supermarkets are not best equipped to deal with.

Cheese, however, continues to hold a special place in the heart of the French. Small specialist shops abound, as do cheese-stalls in local markets, and as yet people are still prepared to take the trouble to find good versions of their favourite cheeses.

BRITISH CHEESES

There is a long history of cheesemaking in Britain. For centuries certain areas of Britain were noted for the cheeses which were made there. The 20th century, however, has seen a marked decline in traditional, farmhouse cheesemaking. The roots for this decline can be traced back to the 19th century, when increased industrialisation saw England's first large-scale cheese dairy open in Derbyshire in the 1870s. A few decades later World War I, with its catastrophic casualties, saw fewer people return to the countryside to pursue traditional skills.

Right: Cheddar is the best-known English cheese

During the 1930s farmers banded together in a co-operative movement to found the Milk Marketing Board. Its aims were to offer a secure market for farmers' milk so that they were not so vulnerable to market forces and large-scale milk buyers forcing down the prices. With this new secure market for surplus milk, guaranteed prices and organised transport, the incentive to make cheese from excess milk lessened considerably.

A few years later saw the outbreak of World War II. Food production fell under the auspices of the Ministry of Food, founded in 1939. The ministry decided that all milk available for cheese should be

Specialist cheese shop display

taken to factories and turned into hard cheeses. There was to be no cheesemaking on the farms. The thinking behind this was to ensure that milk – a precious, protein-rich food-source – be used to the best effect. Its impact, however, was devastating to British farmhouse cheesemaking. After the war only a fraction of former cheesemakers returned to the farms to continue their trade. It has been estimated that before World War II there were 15,000 cheesemakers in Britain, but by the time the war had ended this figure had dwindled to only 126.

Factory-produced versions of British cheeses became the norm during the 1960s and 1970s and only a few cheesemakers continued to make traditional cheeses. Again, the new supermarkets and their preference for mass-produced cheese made on a large scale meant that these small producers had an increasingly difficult time finding an outlet for their stock. A long-standing British deference to French food meant that, ironically, it was far easier to find obscure French cheeses in British delicatessens but not farmhouse versions of great British cheeses.

During the 1980s, however, a handful of enlightened cheese-sellers set about tracking down traditional farmhouse cheeses and offering their makers a retail outlet. Simultaneously, a whole generation of 'new' cheesemakers moved to the countryside and began experimenting with handmade cheeses. The growth in the market for quality British cheese, both traditional and modern, has encouraged both specialist cheese shops and cheesemakers. In 1989 the Specialist Cheesemakers' Association was founded to promote the preservation of traditional cheeses as an important part of our food heritage.

MILK – THE STARTING POINT

Talk to any cheesemaker and the quality of milk used to make cheese comes up as a key matter.

Pasteurisation of milk, where milk is heat-treated to kill off all bacteria, is a subject which arouses deep passions among cheesemakers, both for and against it. With bulk-tanker collection of milk from many farms, carried over considerable distances to various factories, pasteurisation is an efficient and important way of ensuring hygiene.

Many of Europe's small-scale cheesemakers, however, use raw or unpasteurised milk, with much of it coming from their own herds of cattle or produced on farms nearby. They claim that the cheese made from unpasteurised milk has a richer, wider range of flavours than that made from pasteurised. The Kirkham family, for example, famous for their traditional farmhouse Lancashire cheese, use unpasteurised milk from their own herd. This intimate

Cheddar is made from cow's milk

knowledge of the milk that is being used is seen as a vital part of the process of good cheesemaking. The varying flavours of unpasteurised milk are seen by some cheesemakers as key to making fine cheese. Traditionally the best cheeses are made from spring and summer milk, when the livestock is grazed on fresh grass and flowers rather than winter silage.

Cow's milk

Cow's milk is the most commonly used milk in cheesemaking. Dairy cattle lactate for 10 months a year, and by staggering calving, a herd can produce milk all year round.

The majority of milk produced in the United Kingdom comes from herds of Friesian cattle, but some cheesemakers use the richer, creamier milk from Jersey cattle.

Goat's milk

Goats have always been prized for their ability to thrive on difficult terrain; unlike cattle they don't require lush pasture. They have a high milk yield, but a short lactation period. Traditionally goat's cheeses have been seasonal, available when goat's milk is plentiful from spring to autumn.

Goat's milk is free of many of the pathogens found in cow's milk and is hardly ever pasteurised. Although the milk has a high fat content the globules of fat are much smaller than those found in cow's milk. These give the milk a distinct texture and also produce a characteristic white cheese. It is also thought that these small fat globules can be broken down far more easily by our bodies. Increased awareness of lactose intolerance, an adverse human reaction to milk products, has also created renewed interest in goat's cheeses.

When making cheese from goat's milk it requires either more rennet or twice the coagulating time as that of cow's in order to produce the same strength curd.

Sheep's milk

Like goats, sheep can cope with thin pasture which would be inadequate for dairy cattle. The milk contains nearly 10 per cent less water than either cow's or goat's milk, making a much higher yield of cheese per gallon of milk. The milk is rich in fat, which means that the whey from sheep's milk is also high in fat and has historically been used to make whey cheeses such as ricotta. Like goat's milk, the fat in sheep's milk is in very small, fine globules. Again, with a new awareness of lactose intolerance, sheep's milk cheeses are growing in popularity.

Rennet

Rennet, a coagulating agent found in calves' stomachs, has been used to coagulate and curdle cheese for centuries. Its properties are thought to have been discovered when milk was carried in bags made from calves' stomachs.

Historically, however, other vegetarian curdling agents have also been used. Moses' Biblical injunction 'Thou shalt not seethe a kid in his mother's milk' meant that calves' stomach rennet could not be used by the Hebrews. Instead, they resorted to vegetable substances which had coagulant properties, such as thistle buds or fig-tree sap. In England the wild flower Our Lady's Bedstraw, commonly known as Cheese Rennet, was used to curdle milk and to colour Cheshire and Gloucester cheeses. In Portugal there is a strong tradition of using vegetable rennets, from plants such as cardoons.

The use of vegetarian rennets has led to what is called 'vegetarian cheese'. Vegans, however, avoid all cheese, as the system by which surplus milk for human consumption is produced means killing the male calves, kids and lambs.

Recently, concern was aroused when it was realised that vegetarian rennets such as chymosin were created using genetically modified (GM) elements. These rennets were first developed in the 1980s, transferring the DNA material for the enzyme chymosin, which occurs in animal rennet, to dairy yeasts and moulds. The resulting chymosin was then purified so that no DNA fragments were retained. In the face of current consumer concern over any GM traces in food, many cheesemakers are now using vegetarian rennets that have not been genetically modified.

With a growing market for organic foodstuffs developing, there is also a new trend in Britain to produce more organic cheeses, made from organic milk (now increasingly available) and using non-GM rennet.

THE MAGIC OF MOULD

Mould plays a large and important part in cheesemaking. This is less surprising than it first seems if one remembers that cheese is a fermented food, produced by allowing milk to decompose. The skill of cheesemaking is that it channels that process of decomposition to produce a delicious edible foodstuff, just as winemakers work with decomposing grapes to produce wines. Today we live in an age increasingly obsessed with eliminating all bacteria and microbes, so it is worth remembering that there are good bacteria as well as harmful ones.

Mould is an essential part of cheesemaking

Cheesemakers encourage the growth of specific bacteria in order to produce certain flavours and effects. Blue-veined cheeses such as Roquefort or Stilton, with their rich spicy flavours, are the most famous 'mouldy' cheeses. It is generally thought that such blue cheeses were discovered by accident, when ordinary cheeses developed mould and it was discovered how delicious they actually were.

Historically blue cheeses have been matured in damp places, such as caves or cellars, which encourage the growth of mould. Such is the case with France's best-known blue-veined cheese Roquefort, which is mentioned as early as Roman times by Pliny. Roquefort's history has always been closely associated with the local caves. In 1411 Charles VI granted the people of Roquefort the monopoly of maturing the cheese in their caves. These caves are naturally ventilated by vertical fissures called 'fleurines'. The wind blows through the fleurines and picks up tiny *Penicillium roqueforti* spores and blows them over the cheeses which are placed in the caves. Nowadays the making of Roquefort includes piercing the cheese with needles and letting the mould grow throughout the cheese. Once the mould is well-established the cheese is wrapped in foil in order to encourage the mould to grow and to cut out contact with the air.

Stilton, Britain's most famous blue cheese, is another historic cheese, dating back to at least the 18th century. The milk is mixed with starter, *Penicillium roqueforti* and the curds, then cut and ladled into cheese-moulds. The cheese is turned during maturing and then pierced at five to seven weeks old to supply the mould with extra air and encourage its growth. As the cheeses mature they develop a natural, brownish rind.

It is not only in blue-veined cheeses that mould plays a part. The distinctive white bloomy coat found on Camembert and Brie is from the *Penicillium* mould. The curds are drained in highly humid conditions to encourage the growth of the mould. Traditionally, this would have been a naturally occurring mould. Today, however, factories resort to spraying a diluted mould over the maturing cheeses or injecting them into the cheese. The mould works to produce the rind and the cheese's soft, oozy texture and characteristic flavour.

Washed-rind cheeses, such as Munster, with their distinctive orange-red rinds and pungent aromas, are also created through skilful use of moulds. These cheeses are washed and wiped with salt-brine or alcohol during maturation in a warm, humid atmosphere to foster the growth of the correct orange-red bacteria and discourage other, damaging ones.

FARMHOUSE CHEESES

The term 'farmhouse' in this book, when applied to British cheeses, means artisanal cheese, produced by small-scale producers often using unpasteurised milk from either their own herds or from local sources.

One of the interesting things about these artisanal cheeses is that they vary in flavour; the difference between one batch and another might be slight or pronounced. These differences might occur because the livestock have been grazed in different pasture or because the milk has different qualities at different times of the year. With unpasteurised milk the differences are more pronounced. The milk obtained after cows have grazed on a rainy day, for example, will have different qualities to that from cows grazed on a warm, sunny day.

Each batch of artisanal cheeses varies in flavour

Seasonality is another characteristic of these cheeses. Some cheesemakers give their herds a rest from lactating during the winter months because they feel that winter milk is simply not good enough to make good cheese. Soft goat's cheeses, in particular, become very scarce during the winter when traditionally goat's milk is in low supply. In France there is a tradition that goat's cheeses are eaten from Easter to All Saints' Day in November.

One of the reasons that traditional cheeses cost more than mass-produced ones is because of shrinkage.

Plastic-wrapped block cheeses do not breathe and, therefore, do not shrink. A traditional hard, pressed, cloth-wrapped cheese acquires a rind which, while protecting the cheese from air, allows the moisture within the curd to escape into the atmosphere and thus cause the cheese to shrink. Maturing cheeses properly takes skill and care and, therefore, has implied labour costs.

CHOOSING CHEESE

When one thinks of the hundreds of different cheeses that exist, ranging from delicate young soft sheep's milk cheeses to mellow, granular Parmesan, it is a great shame that most of us are creatures of habit, sticking firmly to a few tried and tested favourites such as Cheddar or Brie. If you like a firm Cheddar, then why not try a French Comte, with its sweet rich nuttiness? You may have had a bad experience with an overly strong or pungent blue cheese, yet there are mild versions to be found. Goat's cheese, for example, can range from mild, fresh young cheeses to pungent, distinctly 'goaty' creations such as matured Crottin de Chavingnol.

BUYING CHEESE

A good specialist cheese shop run by helpful, knowledgeable enthusiasts is the most pleasant environment in which to discover more about cheese. A good shop will keep the cheeses in appropriate temperatures and have a fast turnover of stock,

Many specialist cheese shops allow you to taste samples

ensuring that the cheese on offer is fresh and in good condition. Shops such as these stock a wide range of cheeses and also make a point of hunting out artisanal cheeses, made by small producers using traditional methods. These might be 'new' cheeses created by their makers or farmhouse versions of classic cheeses such as Lancashire and Cheshire. The difference in flavour and texture between a cloth-wrapped matured Cheddar carefully made by specialist cheesemakers and a piece of plastic-wrapped mass-produced block Cheddar which hasn't been allowed to develop a rind is quite a revelation.

Stored cheeses

Taste is a notoriously subjective affair and describing a cheese's taste can be surprisingly difficult. The way to discover whether you like a cheese or not is simply to taste it, and the majority of good cheese shops are happy to offer tastings so that the customer can discover for him or herself exactly what the cheese is like. This is especially important with artisanal cheeses, as these will vary in flavour according to a number of factors, from maturity to the season in which they are made. Once you've chosen which cheese you wish to buy, a block should be expertly and freshly cut to order for you.

If there are no such specialist cheese shops near you then supermarkets today offer a much wider selection of cheeses than they used to, particularly those with a delicatessen counter.

Only buy as much cheese as you think you need, as storing cheese in the refrigerator will cause it to dry out very quickly.

STORING CHEESE

Ideally most cheese should be stored in a cool place, such as a larder. Nowadays, however, very few dwellings have such a thing and the refrigerator is used. Chilling cheeses too much, however, takes away their flavour and the airless atmosphere affects their texture and causes them to dry out. Wrap your cheese in several layers of waxed paper or foil and keep it in the lowest and warmest part of the refrigerator. Blue cheese, in particular, should be well-wrapped as the mould is prone to spread.

A whole cheese, especially a whole blue cheese, which is being stored for some time should be turned over every now and then to spread the moisture through the cheese and prevent a 'soggy bottom'.

SERVING CHEESE

For table cheeses which you plan to eat on their own rather than to use in cooking **it is vital that you bring them out of the refrigerator for at least an hour before you plan to eat them**. This is to allow their flavours to come through again, as chilling always dulls the taste of cheese.

In France cheeses are served after the main course and before the dessert, which has the advantage of keeping your palate in savoury mode. This custom also works on the assumption that the wine served with the meal would also go with the cheeses.

ASSEMBLING A CHEESEBOARD

A cheeseboard can be either a delicious, leisurely way to round off a meal or it can be a light meal in its own right. When choosing cheeses to make up a cheeseboard concentrate on quality rather than quantity. One really good cheese, for example a splendid piece of farmhouse

A tempting selection of sheep's and goat's cheeses

Lancashire or a farmhouse Camembert, would make a delicious cheese course on its own.

Presenting three or four cheeses, however, gives you a chance to offer a range of textures and flavours. A classic cheeseboard offers a combination of textures and strengths, starting with a mild fresh soft-textured cheese, perhaps a young chèvre, moving through two contrasting textured cheeses, perhaps a white bloomy rind cheese and a semi-soft cheese and ending with a stronger more powerful cheese. Traditionally blue-veined cheeses are eaten last, as their strong piquant flavour will overpower the other cheeses.

With an increased range of sheep's and goat's cheeses now available, it is possible to assemble a cheeseboard of varying styles made solely from either sheep's or goat's milk: British goat's cheeses to choose from range in flavour from clean, fresh-tasting Perroche or Innes Button to smooth, tangy Tymsboro' or rich Harbourne Blue, while British sheep's cheeses include mould-ripened Flower Marie (with its white bloomy rind), semi-hard Wigmore and a rich, piquant Beenleigh Blue.

More elaborate cheeseboards might offer a goat's cheese, a pressed curd cheese, a hard-pressed cheese, a blue cheese, a washed rind cheese and a downy mould rind cheese.

WHAT TO EAT WITH CHEESE

A good loaf of bread is a reliable accompaniment, allowing the flavour of the cheese to come through and refreshing the palate. Vary the bread according to the cheese: a light, delicate flavoured bread will set off a light delicate cheese while a richer cheese can take a more robust bread such as a sourdough. Alternately, serve good oatcakes or wafers, if you can find some which are not too salty. Butter is an optional extra; if you want to include it, serve an unsalted butter which will allow the flavour of the cheeses to come through clearly.

Fresh fruit, of course, is another classic accompaniment. Apples go well with hard-pressed cheeses such as Cheddar, while pears are often served with blue-veined cheeses. Muscat grapes and figs go well with Pecorino. Walnuts and celery are excellent with blue cheeses. A good homemade chutney which is not too strong can be served with a mature hard cheese. In Spain small squares of sweet *membrillo* (quince paste) are often served with cheese such as Manchego. Similarly, look out for English 'fruit cheeses', made from cooking down fresh fruit and sugar until it reaches a thick set consistency. Dried muscatel raisins, unsulphured dried apricots or dried figs are another delicious accompaniment.

WHAT TO DRINK WITH CHEESE

For many people, wine would be the obvious answer. In France, with its rich tradition of winemaking, cheese and wine are seen as obvious partners. Indeed, such is their perceived indivisibility that cheese, wine and bread are nicknamed the 'Holy Trinity' of the table.

The trick is to find wines which go well with but do not overwhelm the cheese. On the other hand some cheeses will simply dominate the wine. A general principle

Avoid refrigeration

is to serve crisp, fruity wines with lighter fresh-tasting cheeses and fruity, full-bodied wines with stronger cheeses. A mature Cheddar can take a spicy red such as a Chateauneuf-du-Pape or even an oloroso sherry. Red wine tends to be thought of as the classic partner for cheese but, in fact, many white wines set cheese off just as well. Try serving a Sauvignon Blanc or a buttery California Chardonnay with goat's cheese or an Orvieto with Pecorino. In Germany, a fruity Gewürztraminer is served with washed rind cheeses.

When it comes to strong-flavoured blue-veined cheeses such as Stilton or Roquefort then the advice is to move to the sweeter end of the wine spectrum: hence, Sauternes is recommended with Roquefort and port, a fortified wine from Portugal, with Stilton. This combination of savoury and sweet works very well.

Do not feel, however, that you have to serve wine with cheese. A good real ale is an excellent accompaniment to a chunk of farmhouse Cheddar, while in Germany beer is served with washed rind cheeses. In Normandy, traditionally an apple-growing area of France, strong, tangy cider rather than wine is drunk with their local cheeses such as Brie.

Again, it all comes back to that subjective matter of taste. Experiment yourself and see what you enjoy drinking with the cheeses that you enjoy eating.

COOKING WITH CHEESE

Because cheese exists in so many varied forms its uses in the kitchen are wide-ranging. Sometimes it is the main defining ingredient, for example, in a gruyère *gougère* or a blue cheese soufflé; sometimes it is simply a finishing touch: a layering of grated cheese on a creamy root vegetable gratin or a sprinkling of grated Parmesan over tagliatelle with Bolognese ragu.

Soft fresh cheeses such as Italian ricotta are wonderfully versatile and across the different regions of Italy ricotta is used a variety of ways. In Tuscany, for example, combined with cooked spinach and flavoured with salt, pepper and a little grated nutmeg it makes an elegant filling for *crespelli alla Fiorentina*, pancakes stuffed with the ricotta-spinach mixture and baked in tomato and béchamel sauce. In Sicily it is used to make Cassata Siciliana, an elaborate dessert concoction of sweetened ricotta, mixed with grated chocolate, candied peel and glacé fruits and pressed into a Marsala-soaked sponge-lined mould.

In British cookery curd cheese, another soft fresh cheese, is used to make savoury roulades, perhaps flavoured with tomato or spinach, while in East European cookery it crops up in rich baked cheesecakes and dumplings. The French make a dainty dessert called *coeur de la crème*, made by draining fromage frais in a heart-shaped mould and serving it with soft fruit such as strawberries or raspberries. Labne, the Middle Eastern cheese made by draining the whey out of yoghurt, is used as a stuffing for *borek*, tiny savoury filo pastry parcels.

When it comes to cooking with mozzarella, the first thing that comes to mind is, of course, pizza. In Naples, the birthplace of pizza, however, *mozzarella in carrozza*, a deep-fried mozzarella sandwich nicknamed 'mozzarella in a carriage', is a popular street-food too. It is also used on slices of bread as a grilled crostini, topped with chopped anchovies and tomatoes. Good quality buffalo mozzarella can be enjoyed as it is, served with ripe tomatoes and a simple dressing of olive oil, freshly grated pepper and a little salt and a few shredded basil leaves.

Blue-veined cheeses, with their distinctive strong spicy taste, are often mixed with either cream or mild soft cheeses to tone down their dominating flavour. For a simple but rich pasta sauce which goes well with gnocchi, gently heat together roughly crushed Gorgonzola with a little melted butter and double cream or milk until the sauce thickens. In France Roquefort is blended with cream cheese to make a cheese dip or mixed with butter and moulded into little balls for a cocktail canapé.

British hard-pressed cheeses, most famously Cheddar, are widely used in a whole array of dishes, whether as a party nibble like cheese straws or in more substantial dishes like cauliflower cheese. Its grating and melting qualities make it ideal for roux-based cheese sauces, cheese pastry and savoury flans.

Welsh goat's cheese

CHEESE LISTS

British Goat's Cheeses: Golden Cross (a mould-ripened soft cheese), Harbourne Blue (a blue-veined cheese), Perroche (a soft cheese), Ribblesdale Superior (a hard cheese), Ticklemore (a hard cheese).

British Sheep's Cheeses: Beenleigh Blue (a blue-veined cheese), Berkswell (a hard cheese), Flower Marie (a mould-ripened cheese), Lanark Blue (a blue-veined cheese), Spenwood (a hard cheese), Wigmore (a semi-soft cheese).

Blue-veined Cheeses: Bleu d'Auvergne (French cow's milk), Cabrales (Spanish cow's milk, sometimes mixed with goat's or sheep's), Devon Blue (English cow's milk), Dunsyre Blue (Scottish cow's milk), Gorgonzola (Italian cow's milk), Roquefort (French goat's milk), Stilton (English cow's milk).

Continental Sheep's Cheeses: Idiazabal (Basque semi-hard cheese), Kefalotiri (Greek sheep's milk), Ossau-Iraty-Brebis-Pyrenées (French semi-hard cheese), Pecorino (Italian hard cheese).

French Goat's Cheeses: Banon à la Feuille, Bouton d'Oc, Chabichou, Crottin de Chavingnol, Valençay.

Grating Cheeses: Cheddar, Grana Padano, Parmesan, Pecorino Romano.

Soft Cooking Cheeses: Cream cheese, curd cheese, quark, ricotta.

AN A-Z OF CHEESES

Abondance

(Tomme d'Abondance)

A pressed French cheese from the Savoie, and characteristic of the region. Made according to AOC regulations, it is produced from the milk of mountain breeds grazed on alpine pasture. The pressed cheese is soaked in brine then allowed to dry naturally. Maturing takes at least 90 days. It is eaten as a table cheese.

Appearance: Orange-brown rind, pale yellow paste
Milk: Cow's
Taste: Fruity sweetness
Texture: Supple
Shape: Disc
Size: 38-43 cm diameter, 7-8 cm high
Weight: 7-12 kg
Fat: 48%

Ardrahan

A semi-soft, washed rind farmhouse Irish cheese, made in County Cork. The Celtic name means 'height of the ferns'. The milk comes from the makers' own herd of pedigree Friesian cattle. It is eaten as a table cheese.

Appearance: Orange-brown rind, pale yellow paste dotted with tiny holes
Milk: Cow's
Taste: Sweet, slightly mushroomy
Texture: Supple
Shape: Disc
Size: 23 cm diameter, 8 cm or 10 cm high
Weight: 300 g or 1.5 kg
Fat: 45%

Appenzeller

A delicate-smelling, semi-hard Swiss cheese, made from unpasteurised milk. The thick hard rind is washed with spices and white wine or cider. Its history dates back to the 8th or 9th century when it was made in the Swiss canton of Appenzell, after which it is named. Eaten as a table cheese or used as a grilling and melting cheese.

Appearance: Orange-brown rind with a rich yellow interior, pocked with a few small round holes
Milk: Cow's

Taste: Fruity
Texture: Smooth, firm
Shape: Cylinder
Size: Varies
Weight: 6-8 kg
Fat: Up to 50%

Banon à la Feuille

A French soft cheese. Each cheese is dipped in eau-de-vie then wrapped in a softened, sterilised chestnut leaf and ripened. It is named after the town of Banon in Provence where the streets are lined with chestnut trees. The cow's milk version is available all year round, the sheep's milk in spring and summer and the goat's milk late spring and summer. Banon au Pebre d'Ai (also called Povire d'Ane or La Sarriete) is a similar cheese, rolled in savoury sprigs. Eaten as a table cheese.

Appearance: A small round cheese, easy to spot because of its distinctive chestnut leaf-wrapped, raffia-tied exterior. The interior is ivory-coloured
Milk: Cow's, goat's or sheep's
Taste: According to age ranges from mild milky with a slight tang to mildly nutty
Texture: Smooth, firm-textured
Shape: Small disc
Size: 6-7 cm diameter, 2.5-3 cm high
Weight: 90-120 g
Fat: 45%

Bavarian Blue

A modern German semi-soft blue cow's milk cheese. Eaten as a table cheese.

Appearance: A white Camembert-type rind, with a pale cream paste with splodges of blue mould
Milk: Cow's
Taste: Spicy
Texture: Creamy
Shape: Cylindrical
Weight: 1 kg
Fat: 70%

Bavarian Smoked Cheeses

See **Rauchkäse** *on page 153.*

Beaufort

(also known as Gruyère de Beaufort)

A large, round, hard mountain cheese produced in the Savoie province in the French Alps. The French gourmet Brillat-Savarin called it 'the prince of Gruyères'. It is made according to Appellation d'Origine Controllée standards which guarantee that it is produced in a region following established methods.

The cheese is made from the milk of Tarentaise cattle, an ancient breed which in spring are taken high into the mountains to graze in the alpine meadows. The best is Beaufort de Montagne or Beaufort Haute Montagne, made from summer milk in Beaufort, Haute Tarentaise and the Col de la Madeleine-en-Maurienne. Eaten as a table cheese.

Appearance: Hard yellowish rind. With seasonally-produced Beaufort the interior ranges in colour from white in the winter cheese to pale yellow in the summer one
Milk: Cow's
Taste: Ranges from floral to rich, sweet nuttiness
Texture: Smooth, firm and supple
Shape: Wheel
Size: 35-75 cm diameter, 11-16 cm high
Weight: 20-70 kg
Fat: 48%

Beenleigh Blue

A farmhouse blue-veined cheese made from unpasteurised milk using non-GM vegetarian rennet in a similar way to French-style blue cheeses. It is aged for between four and eight months. Eaten as a table cheese.

Appearance: Foil-wrapped pale cream-coloured paste, patched with blue-veining
Milk: Cow's
Taste: Rich, full
Texture: Slightly crumbly
Shape: Cylindrical
Size: 18 cm diameter, 11 cm high
Weight: 3 kg
Fat: 45%

Bel Paese

An Italian semi-soft cow's milk cheese, first made by Egidio Galbani in 1906. Its name means 'beautiful place' in Italian, after a book of the same name written by Abbot Antonio Stoppani, a close friend of the Galbani family, whose portrait appears on the cheese's wrapping. It is now widely exported.

Bel paese is eaten as a table cheese with crackers or bread. It makes tasty *panini* (Italian sandwiches), combined with finely sliced mortadella in focaccio or ciabatta bread.

Appearance: A dark yellow rind with a pale yellow interior
Taste: Mild and sweet
Milk: Cow's
Texture: Soft and creamy
Shape: Wheel
Weight: 2 kg
Fat: 52%

Berkswell

A hard farmhouse cheese made in a 16th-century farmhouse in Berkswell in the West Midlands. The unpasteurised milk used for the cheese comes from the makers' own herd of Friesland sheep. Serve as a dessert cheese or use it, like Pecorino Romano, as a grating cheese, excellent over pasta.

Appearance: Orange-brown hard rind, marked with the weave of the basket in which its pale yellow paste is drained

Milk: Sheep's
Taste: Rich, sweet
Texture: Firm
Shape: Rounded basket
Weight: 3.25 kg

Bleu d'Auvergne

A strong-smelling French semi-soft blue cheese made in the Massif Central in the province of Auvergne according to AOC regulations. Some cheese is still made on mountain farms from unpasteurised milk, but the majority is made in commercial dairies using pasteurised milk. Serve as an after-dinner cheese with red wine or use in canapés or salad dressings, with, for example, a spinach and walnut salad.

Appearance: A thin-rinded cheese (sold foil-wrapped) with a pale creamy paste, evenly spread with dark blue veining
Milk: Cow's
Taste: Piquant, tart
Texture: Moist and sticky
Shape: Cylinder and block
Size: 10 cm diameter, varying height; and 20 cm diameter, 8-10 cm high
Weight: 350 g-1 kg and 2-3 kg
Fat: 45%

Boursault

(also called Lucullus)

A French soft cheese made commercially in the Île de France, invented in the 1950s. It is a triple cream cheese, meaning that cream is added during production, giving the cheese's characteristic subtle creamy flavour. It has a delicate thin rind of white *Penicillium* mould and is matured for two months. It over-ripens very easily so should be discarded if the rind is very red or the cheese is runny. Eaten as a table cheese.

Appearance: A bloomy white rind with a tinge of pink, ivory paste
Taste: Creamy with a slight acidity
Texture: Soft and creamy
Shape: Disc
Size: 8 cm diameter, 4 cm high
Weight: 200 g
Fat: 70%

Boursin

An industrially produced French triple cream cheese from Normandy, invented in the 1950s. Flavoured versions include garlic and herbs or black pepper. Foil-wrapped and boxed, it is popular both in France and abroad. A soft spreadable cheese, it is served with crackers or bread, or used as a filling for baked potatoes.

Appearance: Soft creamy-white paste, flecked with green herbs or black pepper if flavoured
Taste: Depends on flavouring
Texture: Soft, melting
Shape: Disc
Size: 6 cm diameter, 3 cm high
Weight: 80 g
Fat: 70%

Bouton d'Oc

A small, soft, mild cheese, ripened quickly over a 10-day period. Traditionally enjoyed as an aperitif snack with a glass of champagne or sparkling wine.

Appearance: Distinctive pear shape with a straw sticking out through the top, white bloomy rind, ivory paste
Milk: Goat's
Taste: Mild
Texture: Fine
Shape: Pear-shaped
Size: 3 cm diameter base, 1 cm diameter top, 3.5 cm high
Weight: 15 g
Fat: 45%

Brie

A famous soft unpressed cheese, originally from the Île de France but now widely made throughout France and in other countries, including England. Industrial versions are made from pasteurised milk, while farmhouse Bries are made from unpasteurised milk. Such is its popularity that there are several types of Brie. The classic is Brie de Meaux, made according to AOC regulations in the Île de France and reputedly tasted by the Emperor Charlemagne at the Priory of Rueil in Brie. Other Bries include: de Melun (a very fruity-flavoured AOC cheese) and de Montereau (a reddish rind, strong-smelling with a fruity flavour), eaten as a table cheese and also used in canapés and vol-au-vents.

Appearance: A white bloomy rind with a creamy-yellow paste
Taste: Slightly mushroomy with an ammonia tang
Texture: Soft, creamy

Shape: Flat disc
Size: 36-37 cm diameter, 3-3.5 cm high
Weight: 2.5-3 kg
Fat: 45%

Brillat-Savarin

A French soft triple cream cheese with a slight odour of mould. Now factory-produced, it was originally created in the 1930s by Henry Androuet and named after the acclaimed 18th-century French food writer Brillat-Savarin. Avoid if it has a dried-out surface. Eaten as a table cheese or used to make spreads for canapés or sandwiches.

Appearance: A white bloomy rind with a soft cream-coloured paste
Taste: Creamy with a slight sour tang
Texture: Buttery
Shape: Thick disc
Size: 12-13 cm diameter, 3.5-4 cm high
Weight: 450-500 g
Fat: 75%

Brin d'Amour

A fine-textured, dryish Corsican cheese from the mountainous Niolo region, traditionally an area where herds of semi-wild goats roam. The herb coating imparts an aromatic flavour to the cheese which is ripened for one to three months. Fleur de Marquis is a similar cheese, whose name refers to the island's wild flowers. Eaten as a table cheese.

Appearance: Grey rind coated with rosemary and savoury sprigs, bright white paste
Milk: Goat's
Taste: Aromatic
Texture: Firm
Shape: Square with rounded corners
Size: 13 cm square, 4 cm high
Weight: 600 g
Fat: 45%

Bruder Basil

A traditionally made Bavarian smoked cheese, characteristic of German cheeses, also available in a version flavoured with ham. Eaten as a table cheese, grilled or in sandwiches.

Appearance: Dark brown waxed rind, yellow paste with small holes
Milk: Cow's
Taste: Buttery with smoky tang
Texture: Firm
Shape: Block
Weight: 1 kg
Fat: 45%

See also **Rauchkäse** *on page 153.*

Cabecou

(Rocamador)

A type of small French farmhouse soft cheese, produced in the Aquitaine, traditionally between April and November when goat's milk is plentiful. The name comes from Langue d'Oc, the old language of Southern France, and means 'little goat'. Cabecou de Rocamador is made to AOC regulations. Picadou is a strong-tasting cheese produced by wrapping a ripe Cabecou in leaves, spraying it with marc brandy and preserving it in pots. Eaten as a table cheese or grilled.

Appearance: Bloomy white or yellow brown rind, pale white paste
Milk: Goat's or sheep's or a mixture of the two
Taste: Nutty

Texture: Creamy
Shape: Disc
Size: 4-5 cm diameter, 1-1.5 cm high
Weight: 30-40 g
Fat: 45%

Caboc

A soft Scottish double cream cheese, made without rennet and rolled in toasted pinhead oatmeal. The recipe dates back to at least the 15th century when it was the traditional Scottish chieftain's cheese. Pioneering postwar cheesemaker Susanna Stone began making the cheese once again at her creamery in Tain, using an ancient family recipe traced back to her ancestor Mariota de Ile, daughter of The Macdonald, Lord of the Isles. The name comes from the Scots word *kebbuck*, meaning any round cheese. In Scotland it is eaten as a table cheese with oatcakes or spread on a herring fillet and grilled.

Appearance: A grey oatmeal coating with a cream-coloured paste
Milk: Cow's
Taste: Creamy with a mild tang
Texture: Soft, buttery
Shape: Log
Size: 10 cm long, 5 cm high
Weight: 110 g
Fat: 67%

Cabrales

(Cabaliego)

Spain's best-known blue-veined cheese is a strong-smelling semi-hard cheese. Made in mountain farms in Asturias, in the area around Cabrales, the cheese was traditionally wrapped in maple leaves (nowadays foil is generally used instead) and matured in damp limestone caves. Serve as a dessert cheese.

Appearance: Greyish-red crusty rind with a dull white paste patched with yellow-brown splotches and blue-brown veining
Milk: Cow's, sometimes mixed with goat's or sheep's
Taste: Pungent
Texture: Soft, crumbly
Shape: Cylinder
Size: Varies
Weight: 1-5 kg
Fat: 44%

Caciotta

A generic term used to describe a particular type of small, flat semi-soft Italian cheese made throughout Italy. Commercially produced caciotta is made from pasteurised cow's milk and is blander than the farmhouse versions, which can be made from cow's, goat's or sheep's milk or a mixture. Eaten as a table cheese. In Tuscany, Caciotta Toscana is traditionally eaten with young, fresh broad beans.

Appearance: A firm rind with a pale yellow paste
Milk: Cow's, goat's, sheep's or a mixture of all three
Texture: Creamy
Taste: Ranges from sweet to piquant
Shape: Varies
Size: Varies
Weight: Varies
Fat: 42%

Caerphilly

Originally made in Wales in the 1800s, this semi-hard cheese is now produced in England and Wales. A mild cheese, it has always been valued for its digestible qualities. Traditionally eaten young, it used to be known as 'new cheese' in Wales. Because Caerphilly was not long-lasting, the making of it was banned during World War II and it is only recently that Caerphilly production has resumed in Wales. Eaten as a table cheese or used as a melting cheese in dishes like cheese on toast.

Appearance: A thin dark-yellow rind with cream-coloured paste pocked with small holes
Milk: Cow's
Texture: Flaky
Taste: Fresh, salty, slightly lemony
Shape: Cylinders and blocks
Size: Varies
Weight: 3-4 kg
Fat: 48%

Camembert

Originally from Normandy, this famous, quintessentially French soft cheese is now mass-produced throughout France and in other countries in Europe and the United States.

Marie Harel, a farm woman of Camembert, is credited with inventing the cheese in around 1791. Apocryphally, the cheese's name was given by Napoleon III, who sampled the cheese while travelling through the region and called it after the village from which it came. The cylindrical box in which Camembert is still packed to this day was invented by Monsieur Ridel in 1890. The ability to transport Camembert safely over long distances contributed significantly to the growth of its popularity.

The majority of Camembert is nowadays factory-made from pasteurised milk but a proportion is still made in the traditional way. Clues to French farmhouse origin to look out for on the box are the phrases *lait cru* or *non pasteurise*, *fromage fermier* and VCN (Veritable Camembert de Normandie), with Camembert de Normandie protected by AOC regulations. The best Camembert is reputed to come from Pays d'Auge. It is a classic cheeseboard cheese, best enjoyed after a meal.

Appearance: A white bloomy rind marked by reddish lines with a creamy yellow paste	**Texture**: Supple
Milk: Cow's	**Shape**: Flat disc
Taste: Salty and fruity	**Size**: 10.5-11 cm diameter, 3 cm high
	Weight: 250 g
	Fat: 45-50%

Cantal

(also known as Fourme du Cantal)

A hard, pressed French cheese from the Auvergne region. Made according to AOC regulations, it is thought to be the oldest of French cheeses and was mentioned by Pliny the Elder. Industrially produced Chantal Laitier (made from pasteurised milk) is made all year round, while Cantal Fermier is only made during the summer.

In France it is often served after a meal with wine and fruit. Like Cheddar, to which it is often compared, it is also used in cooking in dishes like gratins and soufflés. Aligot is a dish from the Auvergne in which thinly-sliced Cantal is stirred into freshly-mashed potatoes until melted, forming a smooth puree.

Appearance: A dark yellow rind with an ivory-coloured interior
Milk: Cow's
Taste: Varies according to age, from a mild sweetness when young to a strong nuttiness when well-ripened
Texture: Smooth, close-textured
Shape: Cylinder
Size: 36-42 cm diameter, 35-40 cm high
Weight: 35-45 kg
Fat: 45%

Carré de l'Est

A soft Camembert-type French cheese made from pasteurised milk. Originally from Champagne and Lorraine where it is now mass-produced. There is also a washed rind version. Eat as a dessert cheese.

Appearance: A white downy rind and ivory paste. The washed rind version has an orange rind
Milk: Cow's
Taste: Mild, slightly salty
Texture: Soft and supple
Shape: Square
Size: 8-10 cm square, 2.5-3 cm high
Weight: 300 g
Fat: 45%

Cashel Blue

An Irish farmhouse blue-veined cheese, made in Tipperary and named for the Rock of Cashel. It is made from milk from the maker's own herd of Friesian cows with non-GM vegetarian rennet. As it matures over 8 to 14 weeks, the cheese's texture softens and the flavours develop. Eat as a dessert cheese.

Appearance: Thick brown rind, pale yellow paste splotched with blue veining
Milk: Cow's
Taste: Sweet and full with a salty tang
Texture: Firm and moist, becoming creamier as it matures
Shape: Cylinder
Size: 11-16 cm diameter, 15-16 cm high
Weight: 1.5 kg
Fat: 45%

Celtic Promise

A Welsh farmhouse washed rind, semi-soft cheese, made in Carmarthenshire. The drained curds are brine-washed to encourage the growth of the orange moulds which give the cheese its distinctive colour and flavour. Eat as a table cheese.

Appearance: Orange-red sticky rind, yellow paste
Milk: Cow's
Taste: Spicy
Texture: Supple
Shape: Cylinder
Size: 18 cm diameter, 9 cm high
Weight: 500 g

Chabis

(Chabichou)

A small French soft cheese from Poitou, an important goat-breeding region of France. The name comes from a local dialect word for 'goat'. Usually shaped like a truncated cone but also cylindrical. Chabichou du Poitou, made according to AOC regulations, has a thin rind of mould and a soft ivory-coloured paste with a sweet flavour.

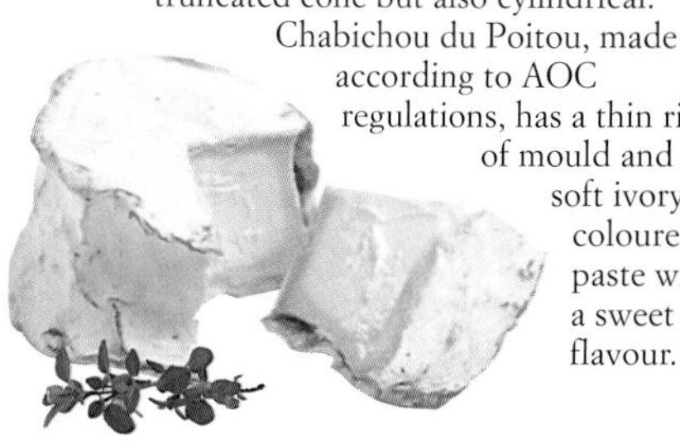

Appearance: A bloomy rind, ranging in colour from white to dark grey
Milk: Goat's
Taste: Ranges from fruity to sharp
Texture: Firm

Shape: Truncated cone, cylinder
Size: 6.5 cm base, 5 cm top, 5-7 cm high
Weight: 120 g
Fat: 45%

Chaource

AOC regulations require this soft French cheese to be made within specified areas of Bourgogne and Champagne. It is eaten very young, at either two to three weeks when semi-cured or one to two months when cured. It is named after the chief town of the canton of Aube. Once wrapped in lettuce leaves to protect it during transport, it is now sold paper-wrapped.

Appearance: A white downy rind and ivory paste
Milk: Cow's
Taste: Milky, fruity
Texture: Smooth, creamy and supple
Shape: Cylinder
Size: 9 cm diameter, 6-7 cm high; 11 cm diameter, 5-6 cm high
Weight: 250 g or 450 g
Fat: 50%

Cheddar

Best-known of all the English cheeses, this hard, pressed cheese has suffered from mass production and imitation. Indeed, it is now widely produced all around the world.

The cheese takes its name from the village of Cheddar on the edge of the Mendip Hills. Its long history is thought to have begun in 1586, while the 18th-century writer Daniel Defoe called it 'the best

cheese that England affords, if not that the whole world affords'. Communal pooling of milk to make a few very large cheeses was one of the characteristics of Cheddar-making which continued until World War I. Its distinctive dense texture and slow-ripening properties are due to the process of 'cheddaring': drained curds are cut into blocks, stacked upon each other, then turned to squeeze out as much whey as possible. It is then put through a curd mill, salted, placed in moulds and pressed.

Industrially-produced rindless block Cheddar is sold at various stages of maturity: mild (six months old), mature (9-12 months) and extra-mature (over a year).

A handful of producers in the West Country continue to make fine farmhouse Cheddars in the traditional way, sometimes using unpasteurised milk. Their cheeses are wrapped in cloth 'bandages' which allow them to breathe as they mature.

A good Cheddar is enjoyed in its own right as an after-dinner cheese, often eaten with apples and sweet digestive biscuits. It is also, however, a versatile cooking cheese, used in everything from cheese on toast and macaroni cheese to quiches and soufflés.

Appearance: Golden smooth paste
Milk: Cow's
Taste: Ranges from mild and sweet to rich, sharp and nutty
Texture: Smooth and firm
Shape: Cylinder and block
Size: Varies
Weight: Varies
Fat: 48%

Cheshire

This pressed cheese is Britain's oldest, thought to date back to pre-Roman times. There is an apocryphal Cheshire story that the Romans hanged a cheesemaker at Chester Court for refusing to tell them his recipe. Some farmhouse Cheshire is still made in the traditional way, but the majority is now industrially produced. There are three varieties: white, red and blue. Annatto is added to the white Cheshire to give colour although the flavour is the same, while blue Cheshire has blue mould added to it. Often eaten in its own right, it is also a very versatile cooking cheese.

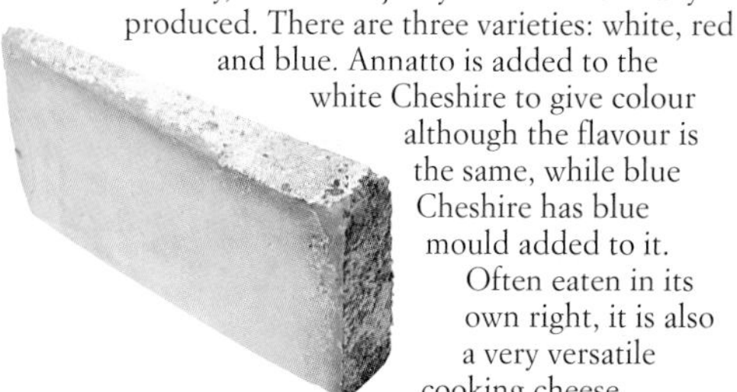

Appearance: White Cheshire is pale cream in colour, red is a pinky-orange colour while blue is pale orange with blue veins
Milk: Cow's
Taste: Salty
Texture: Crumbly, moist
Shape: Cylinder and block
Size: Varies
Weight: Varies
Fat: 48%

Chèvre

Chèvre is the French generic term for goat's cheese. By law French cheeses described as chèvre or pur chèvre must be made entirely of goat's milk and contain at least 45% fat. Chèvre, which tend to be small cheeses, are made throughout France in a whole variety of shapes, from rounds to squat pyramids. Depending on the age of the cheese, its taste of goat's cheese can range from mildly tangy to rich and strong. Traditional flavourings include charcoal (which gives a distinctive black appearance) and fresh herbs. Generally, goat's cheeses are in season from Easter to All Saints' Day in November.

Comte

(Gruyère de Comte)

One of France's great cheeses, this is a cooked, pressed cheese from the Franche-Comte region of France. Dairy records report it being made back in the 13th century; today it is one of France's most popular cheeses. AOC regulations ensure that it is still made in the traditional way in the Jura mountains from locally-produced milk. Serve it either at the end of the meal or use it in canapés, fondues, gratins and soufflés.

Appearance: A tough rind, ranging in colour from yellow to brown, with a deep golden paste scattered with round holes varying from the size of a pea to a marble
Milk: Cow's
Texture: Firm and supple
Taste: Savoury, nutty
Shape: Flattened cylinder
Size: 40-70 cm diameter, 9-13 cm high
Weight: 38-40 kg
Fat: 45%

Coolea

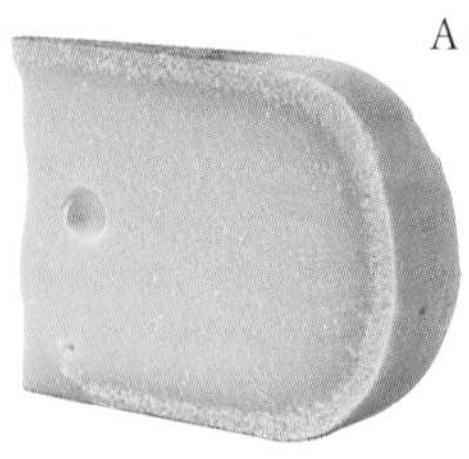

A modern Irish hard-pressed farm cheese made by the Dutch Willens family in County Cork. The Willens use unpasteurised milk, most of it from their own herd. This is a Gouda-style cheese eaten as a dessert cheese at a minimum of six months or up to two years for the large cheeses.

Appearance: Orange rind, dull yellow paste pocked with a few large holes
Milk: Cow's
Taste: Ranges from mild and sweet to deep rich salty-sweetness according to age
Texture: Firm
Shape: Cylinders
Size: Varies
Weight: 1 kg, 2 kg, 4 kg and 10 kg cylinders
Fat: 45%

Cooleney

A modern Irish farmhouse cheese, made in County Tipperary. The milk used is unpasteurised milk from the farm's herd of Friesians. In appearance, it resembles Camembert but has a noticeably thicker rind and moister texture. It is eaten at between four to eight weeks as a table cheese.

Appearance: Thick bloomy white mould rind, ivory paste
Milk: Cow's
Taste: Full
Texture: Supple-soft

Shape: Disc
Size: 10 cm or 25 cm diameter, 5 cm high
Weight: 200 g or 1.6 kg
Fat: 45%

Cornish Yarg

This English pressed, nettle-wrapped cheese draws on ancient cheesemaking techniques where leaves were used as a wrapping; the nettle leaves encourage the growth of *Penicillium* moulds which ripen the cheese. Nettle cheeses were mentioned in the 17th century. Cornish Yarg, however, was developed in the 1970s by Alan and Jennie Gray, whose name spelt backwards gave the cheese its name. Eat as a table cheese.

Appearance: Powdery grey rind with pale white-cream curd
Milk: Cow's
Taste: Fresh and lemony when young, mellow when mature
Texture: Moist and crumbly
Shape: A truckle and a flat wheel
Size: 15 cm and 25 cm diameter, 7 cm high
Weight: 1 kg and 3 kg
Fat: 45%

Cotherstone

A traditional farmhouse cheese made to an old recipe in County Durham and named after a village in Teesdale. Like other Dales cheeses its history can be traced back to the days of monastic cheesemaking. The cheese is ripened for a minimum of two to three weeks but can be matured for up to two months. It can be eaten as a dessert cheese, in Yorkshire often with fruit cake or apple pie, or used in cooking as a grilling cheese.

Appearance: Cream-coloured rind, patched with white and grey moulds, pale yellow paste
Milk: Cow's
Taste: Mild with a tang
Texture: Firm, crumbly
Shape: Cylinder
Size: Varies
Weight: 500 g to 3 kg
Fat: 45%

Cottage Cheese

A low fat curd cheese made from warmed, skimmed milk. The curds are drained, washed and coated with thin cream. The soft, lumpy texture caused by the heating process is characteristic of the cheese.

It is usually sold prepacked in tubs, either plain or flavoured with herbs, fruits, nuts or vegetables. Its low fat content makes it a favourite with dieters. It is eaten with salad ingredients such as tomatoes, cucumber and lettuce, and it also goes well with fresh peaches, pineapple or ripe tomatoes. Flavoured with chives, it makes a simple filling for baked potatoes and can be used in baked dishes such as quiches and flans.

Appearance: Small white curds
Milk: Cow's
Taste: Mild, fresh
Texture: Moist, granular
Fat: Low

Coulommiers

(Brie de Coulommiers or Brie Petit Moule)

A French soft cheese, made in the Île de France and linked historically to Brie de Meaux. Originally a farm cheese made from unpasteurised milk, this is increasingly made in factories from pasteurised milk. Avoid cheeses where the rind is excessively red or thickly rather than lightly covered with white mouldy bloom or the interior paste is very runny. Eaten after dinner or used in croquettes.

Appearance: White downy rind touched with red, ivory-coloured paste
Milk: Cow's
Taste: Mild and delicate when younger, richer when riper
Texture: Soft and supple
Shape: Flat disc
Size: 21-25 cm diameter, 3 cm high
Weight: 400-500 g
Fat: 45%

Coverdale

A pressed English cheese from the Northern Dales, sold either plain or flavoured with chives. Production had ceased after World War II but a creamery near Coverdale has revived it using an old recipe recorded in 1912. Eaten as a table cheese.

Appearance: Whitish, dense paste
Milk: Cow's
Taste: Mild and creamy with a tang
Texture: Close
Shape: Tall truckles
Size: 10 cm round, 6.5 cm tall; 12.5 cm by 14 cm and 15 cm; 23 cm by 15 cm
Weight: 500 g to 6 kg

Cream Cheese

Soft cheese made from single or double cream. Highly spreadable, it is classically eaten with smoked salmon on bagels. You can buy cream cheese ready flavoured with chives or garlic. In cooking it can be used in cheesecakes and to make short pastry.

Appearance: White	**Texture**: Soft
Milk: Cow's	**Fat**: Varies
Taste: Mild, buttery	

Criffel

A Scottish semi-soft, washed rind cheese made by Loch Arthur Creameries from their own organic, unpasteurised milk. The cheese was first made in 1986, inspired by a request from Scottish cheese-seller Ian Mellis. Emulating French mountain cheeses, Criffel is drained in square baskets, salt brine-washed and sold at six weeks old. Eat as a dessert cheese.

Appearance: Yellowy-tan crust marked by the basket in which it is drained	**Taste**: Spicy
Milk: Cow's	**Texture**: Soft
	Size: 18 cm square
	Weight: 1-1.5 kg

Crottin de Chavingnol

(Chavingnol)

Crottin is French for 'horse dung', which gives a vivid idea of this French semi-soft cheese's appearance and scent. Made in Berry to AOC regulations, the farmhouse version is more strongly flavoured than the softer, milder factory-made one. Traditionally crottin is served grilled, with a salad of bitter leaves.

Appearance: Depending on age, a red-brown to dark-grey rind with dark yellow paste
Milk: Goat's
Taste: Pungent, sharp
Texture: Dry and crumbly
Shape: Flattened ball
Size: 4-5 cm diameter, 3-4 cm high
Weight: 60-110 g
Fat: 45%

Crowdie

A Scottish soft cheese, dating back hundreds of years, revived in the 1960s. Known as *gruth* in Gaelic, the name crowdie means 'curds', as it is a skimmed curd cheese. Traditionally it is a rennet-free cheese, with a distinctive texture from being drained in bags. It is available plain or in flavoured versions, with flavourings ranging from wild garlic and hazelnuts to black pepper. It goes well with oatcakes.

Appearance: White or cream-coloured
Milk: Cow's
Taste: Tangy, sharp
Texture: Soft
Shape: Sold in tubs or rolls

Curd Cheese

Traditionally this unripened soft cheese was made with naturally soured milk but nowadays a lactic starter is used. The curds are then drained and salted. It can be eaten fresh or used in cooking, from savoury dishes such as Polish dumplings to sweet ones like Yorkshire curd tart and baked cheesecakes.

Appearance: Creamy coloured
Milk: Cow's
Taste: Buttery with a slight tartness
Texture: Soft
Shape: Sold in tubs

Danish Blue

A Danish veined cheese, invented to compete with Roquefort. This modern blue cheese is now exported to many countries. Can be used in canapés, dips and salad dressings or added to creamy pasta sauces as a rich flavouring.

Appearance: White paste, thickly veined with blue-green
Milk: Cow's
Taste: Sharp, salty
Texture: Creamy
Shape: Cylinders, rectangles and blocks
Size: Varies
Weight: 3 kg
Fat: 50-60%

Derby

This hard-pressed English cheese was the first to be made in a factory, back in 1870. Traditionally eaten young, when it is extremely mild, its flavour develops when it's allowed to mature. Sage Derby, flavoured with sage juice, is sharper. Eat with apples, pears or grapes or use it as a grilling cheese, for example, in cheese on toast.

Appearance: Pale yellow paste (marbled green when Sage Derby)
Milk: Cow's
Taste: Mild
Texture: Dense
Shape: Cylinder
Size: 30-34 cm across, 8-10 cm deep
Weight: 14 kg
Fat: 48%

Devon Blue

A farmhouse blue-veined sheep's cheese made in Devon from unpasteurised milk and non-GM vegetarian rennet. It is made according to French blue-cheese methods, where *Penicillium roqueforti* is added to the warmed milk to trigger the growth of mould. Once the blue mould has started to develop, the cheese is wrapped in foil to encourage its growth. It is matured for between six and eight months. A table cheese; try serving it with pears to set off its salty-sweetness.

Appearance: Foil-wrapped pale cream-coloured paste, patched with blue-green veining
Milk: Sheep's
Taste: Spicy
Texture: Crumbly
Shape: Cylinder
Size: 18 cm diameter, 11 cm high
Weight: 3 kg
Fat: 45-50%

Devon Garland

A hard-pressed English farmhouse cheese, based on an old West Country cheese and revived in the 1970s by a Devon-based cheesemaker. The picturesque name reflects both the place of origin and the characteristic layer of herbs set in the cheese. It is lightly pressed and ripened for six to eight weeks. Eaten as a table cheese.

Appearance: Grey-brown rind, creamy yellow paste with herb-layer
Milk: Cow's
Taste: Fresh, savoury
Texture: Firm
Shape: Wheel
Size: 22.5 cm diameter, 7.5 cm high
Weight: 4 kg
Fat: 45%

Dolcelatte

(Gorgonzola Dolcelatte)

A factory-made semi-soft, blue-veined Italian cheese, a milder, more digestible version of Gorgonzola characterised by its melting texture. The name means 'sweet milk' in Italian. Eaten as a table cheese or melted over pasta.

Appearance: Blue-veined creamy-coloured paste
Milk: Cow's
Taste: Delicate

Texture: Creamy
Shape: Cylinder
Size: Varies
Weight: 1-2 kg
Fat: 50%

Dorset Blue Vinney

This hard, skimmed milk British cheese practically vanished during the 1970s and has only recently been revived as a farmhouse cheese produced in the county of Dorset. There are apocryphal tales that the cheese's characteristic mould was obtained by dunking old harnesses into the milk. Nowadays, more conventionally, the blueing is caused by adding *Penicillium roqueforti* to the milk. Eaten as a table cheese.

Appearance: Cream or yellow with blue-green veins
Milk: Cow's
Taste: Strong, sharp
Texture: Hard
Shape: Cylinders
Size: Varies
Weight: 1.35-2.3 kg and 6 kg
Fat: 40%

Double Gloucester

This ancient, hard-pressed English cheese became popular in the 18th century. The 'double' of the name is thought to refer either to the fact that milk from two milkings was traditionally used to make the cheese or the thickness of the cheese (twice as thick as Single Gloucester). It is available in both farmhouse and factory-made versions. Annatto is sometimes used to colour the cheese. Eaten as a table cheese or used as a melting and grilling cheese.

Appearance: Pale to deep orange
Milk: Cow's
Taste: Mellow
Texture: Buttery
Shape: Disc
Size: 30 cm diameter, 12 cm high
Weight: 11 kg
Fat: 48%

Dunlop

Sometimes called Scottish Cheddar, this hard-pressed cheese has been made in Scotland since the 17th century, though output fell considerably in the post-World War II years. It has been revived by a farmhouse producer who uses milk from a mixed herd of local cattle from a nearby Ayrshire farm. Like Cheddar, it can be eaten as a table cheese or used in dishes such as cheese on toast.

Appearance: Dark yellow rind, pale yellow paste
Milk: Cow's
Taste: Mellow
Texture: Hard

Shape: Truckles and wheels
Size: Varies
Weight: 200 g, 400 g, 2.5 kg and 20 kg
Fat: 53%

Dunsyre Blue

An unpressed blue-veined farmhouse cheese, from Lanarkshire in Scotland. The maker uses unpasteurised milk and non-GM vegetarian rennet. Penicillium is added into the warmed milk to create the blueing. The cheese is matured for around three months and is eaten as a table cheese.

Appearance: Creamy yellow paste with distinct blue veins
Milk: Cow's
Taste: Mild with a spicy tang, more pronounced as it gets older
Texture: Creamier as it matures
Shape: Cylinder
Weight: 3 kg
Fat: 52%

Durrus

A semi-soft Irish farmhouse cheese made in Durrus in County Cork. Eaten as a table cheese.

Appearance: Pink-brown rind, primrose yellow paste
Milk: Cow's
Taste: Sweet, fruity
Texture: Supple
Shape: Disc
Weight: 375 g and 1.5 kg
Fat: 45%

Edam

Holland's best-known cheese is a semi-hard cheese, named after the town of Edam in which it was originally made. It is now mass-produced all over Holland. The majority of Edam is sold when only a few months old. A black wax coating indicates mature Edam, with a stronger flavour. Cumin seeds are sometimes added for flavouring. Edam's comparatively low fat content makes this a favourite cheese for dieters, served with oatcakes or a salad.

Appearance: Red paraffin wax coating with rich golden yellow paste
Milk: Cow's
Taste: Mild
Texture: Smooth and supple
Shape: Sphere
Size: Varies
Weight: 880 g-6.5 kg
Fat: 40%

Edenpilz

A semi-soft German blue-veined cheese, traditionally eaten as an after-dinner cheese.

Appearance: Ivory paste with fine, dark blue veins
Milk: Cow's
Taste: Strong, fruity
Texture: Melting
Shape: Drum or loaf-shaped
Size: Varies
Weight: 2-5 kg
Fat: 45%

Emlett

A modern English farmhouse soft cheese. The maker uses unpasteurised milk from the farm's own herd of Friesland sheep and traditional rennet. The cheese is aged for between two and four weeks. Eaten as a table cheese.

Appearance: White bloomy rind with rust-coloured patches, white paste
Milk: Sheep's
Taste: Mild, slight tang and nuttiness
Texture: Smooth, soft
Shape: Disc
Size: 7 cm diameter, 3 cm high
Weight: 150 g

Emmenthal

Switzerland's most famous, much-imitated cheese is a huge, pressed cooked cheese, named after the Emme Valley near Bern. The genuine article has 'Switzerland' stamped all over the rind and is made from unpasteurised milk in the mountain cantons. To make one 80 kg cheese takes 1,000 litres of milk. It is eaten as a dessert cheese and used in cooking, classically in fondue where it is melted with white wine and kirsch.

Appearance: Golden paste evenly pocked with round holes
Milk: Cow's
Taste: Mellow, sweet, nutty
Texture: Firm, smooth
Shape: Big wheel
Size: Varies
Weight: 60-130 kg
Fat: 45%

Epoisses

A soft French cheese made in Burgundy. It is first washed with sage and then with Burgundy marc brandy and has a very strong flavour. Admirers include the 18th-century French gourmet Brillat-Savarin, who called it the 'king of cheeses', and Napoleon I. It is also flavoured with cloves, fennel and black pepper. Eaten as a table cheese.

Appearance: Orange rind, light to dark yellow paste
Milk: Cow's
Taste: Tangy, spicy
Texture: Supple

Shape: Flat cylinder
Size: 10 cm wide, 3-5 cm high
Weight: 450 g
Fat: 45%

Feta

A Greek semi-soft cheese, made for centuries in Greece and now widely produced around the world. Authentic Greek feta is made from sheep's milk and has a distinctive tanginess, while commercially produced cow's milk feta is milder. Normally sold pre-packed in brine, drain and rinse it to wash off excessive saltiness. It can be eaten fresh and is also widely used in Greek cooking, from salads to savoury filo pastries (such as *spanokopitta*).

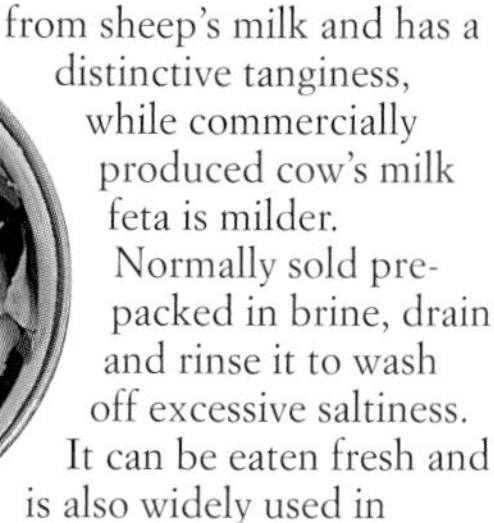

Appearance: Bright white
Milk: Cow's or sheep's
Taste: Salty
Texture: Firm and crumbly
Shape: Blocks
Fat: 50%

Finn

An unpressed English triple cream cheese made by Charles and Grainne Westhead of Neal's Yard Creamery. The name, Celtic for 'White Aged One', is inspired by Grainne's Irish roots and the colour of the cheese but primarily by their much-loved dog. It is made with non-GM vegetarian rennet from unpasteurised milk enriched with 10 per cent of cream. Plans are afoot to make it from organic milk. It was the first of the cheeses produced at Neal's Yard Creamery and is eaten at around two to three weeks. Eaten as a dessert cheese.

Appearance: Thick white rind, ivory paste
Milk: Cow's
Taste: Mild and sweet with a slight tang
Texture: Supple
Shape: Round
Size: 10-12 cm diameter, 4 cm high
Fat: 45%

Flower Marie

A modern, unpressed, mould-ripened English farmhouse cheese made in East Sussex from unpasteurised milk from one herd of sheep. The brined cheeses are ripened for between five and six weeks. It has a delicate flavour, a melting texture and is eaten as a dessert cheese.

Appearance: White bloomy rind, cream-coloured paste
Milk: Sheep's
Taste: Mild when young, tangy when mature
Texture: Densely creamy
Shape: Square
Size: 70-80 cm square
Weight: 200 g min
Fat: 45%

Fontal

Created in Trentino, Italy after World War II, this factory-made semi-hard cheese is often used as a cheaper substitute for fontina in making *fonduta* (a classic Piedmontese sauce made from grated fontina flavoured with white truffles), toasted sandwiches and savoury pies.

Appearance: Ivory white paste with just a few holes
Milk: Cow's
Taste: Mild to fruity
Texture: Supple
Shape: Wheel
Size: 40 cm diameter, 9 cm deep
Weight: 6-20 kg
Fat: 45%

Fontina

A highly-prized, semi-hard Italian cheese made only in the Val d'Aosta in the Italian Alps. It is made from unpasteurised milk, during the summer months in mountain chalets and in small valley factories during winter. Records dating from 1447 show that it was being made in the area at that time.
Italians enjoy it both as an after-dinner cheese and use it in cooking, most famously in *fonduta*, a Piedmontese fondue made from grated fontina, egg yolks and grated white truffle.

Appearance: Thin brown rind with a rich yellow paste with a few differently sized holes
Milk: Cow's
Taste: Delicate sweet nuttiness
Texture: Smooth, slightly supple
Shape: Wheel
Size: 46 cm diameter, 8.5 cm thick
Weight: 9.5 kg
Fat: 45%

Fourme d'Ambert

A French blue-veined cheese produced in the area round Ambert, after which it is named, and protected by AOC regulations. The French word *fourme* derives from the Latin *forma* (mould or shape), from which the word *fromage* (cheese) is thought to come. Blue mould is introduced to the cheese, then air injected through it to help it to spread. Fourme de Montbrison is a similar cheese produced in the same area. Like Stilton it should be sliced horizontally. Eaten as a table cheese.

Appearance: Brown-grey rind, creamy-coloured paste with dark-blue veining
Milk: Cow's
Taste: Savoury, tangy
Texture: Creamy, smooth
Shape: Tall cylinder
Size: 13 cm diameter, 19 cm high
Weight: 1.5-2 kg
Fat: 50%

Fromage Frais

A fresh curd cheese, sometimes enriched with cream, originally made in France and now produced in other countries. It is used in sweet and savoury dishes, for example, to thicken sauces or in quiches. In a classic French dessert it is drained through muslin and eaten with sugar and cream. Try serving it with summer berries, such as strawberries and raspberries, or crystallised fruit.

It is usually made from pasteurised milk, although in France it is possible to find farmhouse versions made from unpasteurised milk. In France there are several regional versions of fromage frais, such as Claqueret Lyonnais flavoured with shallot, garlic and herbs.

Appearance: White and smooth
Milk: Cow's, goat's or sheep's
Taste: Ranges from slightly sharp to rich
Texture: Soft and smooth
Fat: Varies

Gabriel

A farmhouse hard, pressed cheese from West Cork in Ireland. Made from unpasteurised milk, this is in the style of Switzerland's famous mountain cheeses. It has a grainy texture and considerable depth of flavour. It is a slow-ripening cheese, aged for nine months to a year. An excellent table cheese, but also good in fondues.

Appearance: Hard brown rind, deep yellow paste
Milk: Cow's
Taste: Full and savoury with a bite
Texture: Hard, dry, grainy
Shape: Wheel
Weight: 6.85 kg and 27 kg

Gaperon

(Gapron)

A French semi-soft cheese made in the Auvergne and named after the local dialect word for buttermilk. Flavoured with garlic and pepper, it was traditionally cured on a hook by the fire. The number of cheeses hung by the fire used to be an indicator of a farmer's wealth. Eaten as a table cheese.

Appearance: A white bloomy rind and a creamy paste
Milk: Cow's
Taste: Strong with a hint of garlic
Texture: Supple
Shape: An upturned pudding basin
Size: 8-9 cm diameter base, 8-9 cm high
Weight: 250-350 g
Fat: 30-45%

Gjetost

A semi-hard Norwegian whey cheese, which when made entirely from goat's milk is labelled *ekte*, meaning 'genuine'. The distinctive colour and sweet flavour are produced by boiling down the whey until the milk sugar caramelises. In Norway it is eaten at breakfast or with spiced cake at Christmas.

Appearance: Toffee-brown colour
Milk: Cow's and/or goat's
Taste: Sweet
Texture: Firm
Shape: Block
Size: Varies
Weight: 250-500 g
Fat: 38%

Golden Cross

A farmhouse cheese made in East Sussex from unpasteurised milk from the makers' own herd of goats. It's named after the nearest village to the farm.

Laughton Log is a larger version, weighing 1 kg. The cheese is made throughout the year, although larger quantities are produced in late spring to early autumn because of increased milk yields.

Both cheeses are eaten as dessert cheeses or, as they have a firm texture, are excellent grilled.

Appearance: Charcoal-dusted surface, white paste
Milk: Goat's
Taste: Sharp and fresh when young, mellow when mature
Texture: Firm
Shape: Log
Size: 120-130 cm long, 40 cm diameter
Weight: 225 g min
Fat: 45%

Gorgonzola

Italy's best-known blue-veined cheese is one of the world's oldest veined cheeses, dating back over a millennium when it was created in the eponymous village near Milan (now a suburb of the city). Apocryphally, it was invented by accident when a Lombardy innkeeper was given some cheese in payment by travelling herdsmen. Stored in damp cellars the cheese went mouldy but was discovered to taste delicious. Today it is still made in Lombardy, both in farmhouses and factories. Traditionally, the cheese was stored in damp caves to encourage the growth of mould. Nowadays, the cheese is poked with long metal needles to expose the cheese to air and thus help the mould to form, then ripened in a

cool humid atmosphere for three to four months. It should have a sharp clean smell. Avoid buying Gorgonzola that has a sour smell or is brownish or hard.

Classically it is eaten after meals with unbuttered bread or ripe pears. It can also be used to great effect in pasta sauces, such as *quattro formaggi*, or simply melted with a little cream over gnocchi. In Lombardy it is often spread on grilled polenta.

Torta de Gorgonzola is a rich, creamy cheese created by pressing together alternate layers of Gorgonzola and Mascarpone, a combination which originates from the Trieste area.

Appearance: Reddish-grey rind with an ivory paste with greenish-blue marbling
Milk: Cow's
Taste: Spicy to sharp
Texture: Soft, creamy

Shape: Cylinder
Size: 25-30 cm diameter, 15-20 cm high
Weight: 2 kg
Fat: 48%

Gouda

Holland's best-known cheese originated in the town of Gouda in the 13th century. It now accounts for over two-thirds of Dutch cheese production. Although the majority is factory-made, it is still possible to find farmhouse gouda, made by traditional methods from unpasteurised milk. These have the word 'boeren' (from *boer* meaning 'farmer') stamped on the rind. A black-wax coating indicates a mature gouda, with a fuller flavour and firmer texture which is excellent for grating. It can be eaten as it is, with the Dutch enjoying it finely sliced at breakfast time, or used in cooking. When young it is used as a melting cheese.

Appearance: Yellow or black waxed rind, yellow paste with a few holes
Milk: Cow's
Taste: Mild, buttery
Texture: Smooth
Shape: Cylinder
Size: Varies
Weight: 2.5-20 kg
Fat: 48%

Grana Padano

The term *grana* is the generic Italian name for hard, grainy cheeses, the most famous of these being Parmesan which Grana Padano closely resembles. Made in the Po Valley, it ripens more quickly than Parmesan and is sold at different ages. Young Grana Padano (at one year) is moist and mild, while the mature cheese (two years) is drier and has a fuller flavour. Mature Grana Padano makes an excellent, cheaper substitute for Parmesan and is used with pasta dishes.

Authentic Grana Padano has the name stamped all over the rind. Wrapped in foil it keeps well in the refrigerator or for up to five months in the freezer. Use it freshly grated rather than grating it in advance as it quickly loses its flavour.

Appearance: Depending on age: thick ochre or black rind, light to dark yellow paste
Milk: Cow's
Taste: Mild when young, fuller and richer when mature
Texture: Moist and firm when young; hard, crumbly when mature
Shape: Cylinder
Size: Varies
Weight: 24-40 kg
Fat: 32%

Gruyère

A famous Swiss cheese, which like Emmenthal is a pressed cooked cheese. Authentic Gruyère, made in mountain dairies from unpasteurised milk, has the word 'Switzerland' stamped all over the rind. The cheese originated in the town of Gruyère in the 12th century. It is enjoyed as a dessert cheese and is also an excellent cooking cheese, classically used in fondues and sauce Mornay.

Appearance: Red-brown rind, with pale yellow paste speckled with small holes
Milk: Cow's
Taste: Sweet and nutty

Texture: Firm
Shape: Wheel
Size: 61-66 cm diameter, 10 cm thick
Weight: 20-45 kg
Fat: 45%

Gubbeen

An Irish farmhouse semi-soft washed rind cheese made in County Cork. The cheesemakers use unpasteurised milk from the farm's own mixed herd of Jersey, Friesian, Simmenthal and Kerry cattle. Eaten as a table cheese.

Appearance: A pinkish rind, pale yellow paste dotted with holes
Milk: Cow's
Taste: Mellow
Texture: Supple
Shape: Disc
Size: 17 cm diameter, 6 cm high
Weight: 1.5 kg

Halloumi

A Greek cheese, traditionally made from sheep's milk but also from cow's milk, and usually flavoured with shreds of mint. In Greek and Cypriot cookery it is traditionally served as a mezze dish: sliced then grilled over charcoal or fried in oil until golden-brown. It can also be grated on top of moussaka.

Appearance: Ivory-coloured
Milk: Cow's or sheep's
Taste: Salty, milky
Texture: Firm and elastic
Shape: Block
Fat: 40%

Harbourne Blue

A flavourful farmhouse blue-veined goat's cheese produced in Devon. The maker, who specialises in blue-veined cheeses, uses unpasteurised milk and a non-GM vegetarian rennet. French methods are followed, where once the mould has started to grow on the cheeses they are then wrapped in foil to encourage the blueing. Serve as a dessert cheese.

Appearance: White paste spread with blue-green veins
Milk: Goat's
Taste: Piquant
Texture: Creamy
Shape: Cylinder
Size: 10 cm high, 18 cm diameter
Weight: 5 kg
Fat: 48%

Hereford Hop

A hard-pressed farmhouse cheese produced in Dymock, Gloucestershire. The second part of the name refers to the fact that the cheese is matured in a coating of toasted hops, and the label has a picture of a boy hopping. The maker is vague about why it's called 'Hereford', but he did once live close to the border. It can be eaten as a dessert cheese and is also an excellent cooking and grating cheese.

Appearance: A distinctive dark khaki-coloured rind coated with toasted hops
Milk: Cow's
Taste: Flowery
Texture: Moist, firm
Shape: Rounds
Size: 20 cm diameter, 7 cm high
Weight: 2.5 kg
Fat: 45%

Idiazabal

A hard Spanish cheese from the Basque country. Lightly smoked with hawthorn and beech wood, it is ripened in mountain caves. Eaten as a table cheese or used as a grating and grilling cheese.

Appearance: Dark caramel-coloured rind, creamy white paste
Milk: Sheep's
Taste: Smoky, herby
Texture: Firm, waxy
Shape: Cylinder
Weight: 1-3 kg
Fat: 53%

Isle of Mull

A Scottish traditional farmhouse cheese made on the Isle of Mull with unpasteurised milk from the maker's own herd. The cheese is made to a Cheddar-style recipe. Eat as a table cheese or use as a grating and melting cheese as Cheddar.

Appearance: Dark brown rind marked by the cloth in which the cheese was wrapped, pale yellow paste
Milk: Cow's
Taste: Tangy
Texture: Firm
Shape: Cylinder
Weight: 200 g, 400 g, 800 g, 1 kg, 2 kg
Size: Varies

Innes Button

Small, dainty farmhouse soft cheeses made at Highfields in Staffordshire. Innes Cheeses was started by Hugh Lillington, heir to Thorpe Park, to make the estate financially viable. The milk comes from the estate's own herd of goats. This fresh-tasting, light-textured cheese is eaten as a dessert cheese.

Appearance: Tiny round white cheeses, plain or ash- or herb-coated
Milk: Goat's
Taste: Mild and fresh
Texture: Light, smooth
Shape: Small disc
Size: 4.5 cm diameter, 4.25 cm high
Weight: 40 g

Jarlsberg

A classic Norwegian cheese, based on a traditional Norwegian type and re-invented in the 1950s. Factory-made from pasteurised milk, it is a commercial success, much exported around the world. It is eaten as a table cheese or used in cooking as a grilling and melting cheese.

Appearance: Golden yellow paste pocked with differently sized holes
Milk: Cow's

Taste: Sweet, slightly nutty
Texture: Supple
Shape: Cylinder
Weight: 10 kg
Fat: 45%

Kefalotiri

This Greek hard cheese is predominantly grated and used in cooking. The name comes from *kefali*, meaning 'head', which it is supposed to resemble.

Appearance: White to pale yellow paste with irregular-sized holes
Milk: Sheep's
Taste: Fresh, sharp
Texture: Firm
Shape: Cylinder
Size: Varies
Weight: 6-8 kg
Fat: 40%

Lanark Blue

A Scottish farmhouse blue-veined cheese, often compared to Roquefort. Made with unpasteurised milk from the maker's own flock of sheep and non-GM vegetarian rennet, this is a seasonal cheese, made between March and October. *Penicillium* is added to the heated milk to create the characteristic blueing and the moulded cheese is pierced to help the mould develop. The cheese is ripened for around three months. Eaten as a table cheese, it goes particularly well with pears.

Appearance: Grey rind, pale, off-white paste with intense blue veins
Milk: Sheep's
Taste: Sharp, salty and creamy with a pepperiness as it matures
Texture: Creamy
Shape: Cylinder
Size: Varies
Weight: 1.5 kg, 3 kg
Fat: 52%

Lancashire

A traditional hard-pressed English cheese, originally made in Lancashire, dating back to at least the 18th century. A post-World War II decline in farmhouse Lancashire means that the majority of Lancashire today is factory-made. Traditionally-made farmhouse Lancashire has a richer, tangier flavour. Sage Lancashire, originally made for Christmas, is also found. A good dessert cheese which also melts easily, making it excellent for cooking and ideal for Welsh Rarebit.

Appearance: Pale cream-coloured paste	**Texture**: Creamy, crumbly
Milk: Cow's	**Shape**: Tall cylinder
Taste: Mild to strong, depending on age	**Size**: Varies
	Weight: 4-18 kg
	Fat: 48%

Langres

A strong-smelling French washed rind soft cheese from the province of Champagne. Made to AOC regulations, it is brine-washed during ripening to encourage the growth of orange bacteria. Annatto, the vegetable food colouring, is also rubbed on the rind to enhance its colour. There is a characteristic hollow at the top of the cheese into which marc brandy is sometimes poured during maturing to seep into the cheese. Eat as a table cheese.

Appearance: Orange-brown rind, white to cream-coloured paste	**Shape**: Cylinder
Milk: Cow's	**Size**: 7.5-9 cm diameter, 4-6 cm high, 16-20 cm diameter, 5-7 cm high
Taste: Spicy	
Texture: Supple	

Leicester

(Red Leicester)

A hard-pressed British cheese, originally made in Leicestershire and dating back to at least the 18th century. Its distinctive colour comes from Annatto. Nowadays it is mostly produced in factories. A quick-ripening cheese, it is best eaten at between three to six months. Eaten as a table cheese or used as a melting and grilling cheese.

Appearance: Deep orange-red
Milk: Cow's
Taste: Slightly sweet
Texture: Flaky
Shape: Wheel
Size: Varies
Weight: 4-22 kg
Fat: 48%

Leiden

A pressed Dutch cheese, made from a mixture of skimmed milk and buttermilk and flavoured with cumin seeds. Named after the city of Leiden, the cheese is both factory- and farmhouse-made. The sharper farmhouse version has a deep orange-red rind (from Annatto), an orange wax coat if exported, and is stamped with the words 'Boeren Leidse' and a pair of crossed keys, symbolising Leiden. Eaten as a table cheese or used as a grilling cheese.

Appearance: Yellow or orange wax coating, yellow paste flecked with cumin seeds
Milk: Cow's
Taste: Mild with cumin overtones
Texture: Firm
Shape: Cylinder
Size: Varies
Weight: 4-12 kg
Fat: 20-40%

Limburger

A soft washed-rind cheese with a notoriously strong smell. Originally from Belgium, it is produced in other countries, notably Germany. Avoid buying it if the paste is runny or the rind slimy as these are signs of over-ripeness. In Germany it is eaten as a table cheese or melted over potatoes.

Appearance: Reddish-brown skin and yellow paste
Milk: Cow's
Taste: Spicy
Texture: Creamy
Shape: Block
Size: Varies
Weight: 220 g to 1 kg
Fat: 20-50%

Lincolnshire Poacher

A modern farmhouse English Cheddar-type cheese, and the only cheese made in Lincolnshire. The maturing time ranges from 11-12 months for the ordinary cheeses and up to two years for the Vintage. Like Cheddar it can be eaten as it is or used in cooking as a grating or grilling cheese.

Appearance: Dark grey rind, golden paste
Milk: Cow's
Taste: Sweet to tangy depending on age
Texture: Firm
Shape: Truckle
Size: 27 cm diameter, 27 cm high
Weight: 2.3 kg

Little Rydings

A seasonal unpressed English farmhouse cheese made in Avon from unpasteurised milk and traditional rennet. The milk comes from the maker's own herd of Friesland sheep and the cheese matures for three to five weeks. Eat as a table cheese.

Appearance: White bloomy rind, dotted with rust-coloured patches, white paste
Milk: Sheep's
Taste: Full, mushroomy
Texture: Supple-soft
Shape: Disc
Weight: 200 g
Fat: 48%

Livarot

Nicknamed the 'Colonel' because of the stripes wrapped round it, this French soft cheese is one of Normandy's most ancient. It comes from the Calvados region where it is made primarily in farmhouses according to AOC regulations. The rind is coloured with Annatto and the cheese is ripened in a warm humid atmosphere, traditionally cellars. Runniness, a sinking in the middle or a smell of ammonia are signals of over-ripeness. In France it is eaten with cider or Calvados (apple brandy).

Appearance: Brownish-red rind encircled with five thin rush or paper strips, ivory-coloured paste
Milk: Cow's
Taste: Spicy, full-bodied

Texture: Elastic
Shape: Cylinder
Size: 11-12 cm diameter, 4-5 cm high
Weight: 450 g
Fat: 40% min

Llangloffan

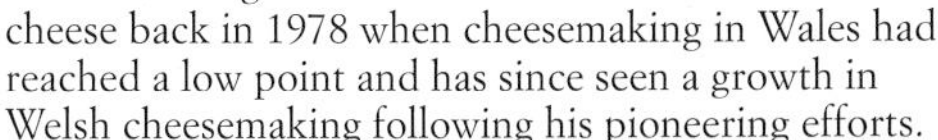

A farmhouse-produced Welsh hard-pressed cheese, made from unpasteurised milk from Jersey, Brown Swiss and Friesian cows. Leon Downey first started making this cheese back in 1978 when cheesemaking in Wales had reached a low point and has since seen a growth in Welsh cheesemaking following his pioneering efforts.

Like Cheddar this is a versatile cheese, eaten either as a dessert cheese or used in cooking. There is also a version flavoured with garlic and chives.

Appearance: Stone-coloured rind, yellowish paste
Milk: Cow's
Taste: Rich, buttery
Texture: Firm, slightly crumbly

Shape: Wheel
Size: Varies
Weight: 1.4 kg, 4.5 kg, 13.5 kg
Fat: 56%

Loch Arthur Organic Farmhouse Cheese

A Scottish hard-pressed cheese made at Loch Arthur Creamery at the Campbell Village Trust in Dumfries. The organic milk for the cheeses comes from their own cows and the cheeses are made in traditional cloth-bound rounds. A Scottish Cheddar-style cheese, it can be eaten as a dessert cheese or used in cooking.

Appearance: The paste varies in colour according to season: a pale chalky yellow in winter to a deeper yellow in summer
Milk: Cow's
Taste: Mild when young, with a distinctive bite when mature
Texture: Firm, slightly granular when mature
Shape: Cylinders
Size: 22.8 cm diameter, 22.8 cm high
Weight: 9 kg
Fat: 48%

Mahon

A soft Spanish cheese, made in the Balearic Islands, notably Menorca. After maturing it is smeared with olive oil to help preserve it. Eaten as a table cheese or grated over pasta.

Appearance: Patchy brown rind with creamy white paste, darkening with age
Milk: Cow's
Taste: Slightly sour
Texture: Creamy paste, hardening with age
Shape: Block
Size: Varies
Weight: 2-4 kg
Fat: 45%

Manchego

Spain's most famous cheese, originally from the plains of Don Quixote's La Mancha, but now made all over the country. Around the sides of the cheese the rind retains the pattern of plaited esparto grass, while the top and bottom are marked by the cheese press. It is sold at three stages of maturity: *fresco* (under three weeks), *curado* (16 weeks) and *anejo* (six months to a year), sometimes in olive oil.

Eat as an appetiser with chorizo or as a dessert cheese, classically with *membrillo* (quince paste). The older cheese is used in cooking as a grating cheese or cubed, coated in beaten egg and breadcrumbs and fried.

Appearance: Yellow rind, with ivory to rich yellow paste marked by a few holes
Milk: Sheep's
Taste: Nutty, buttery
Texture: Elastic to hard, depending on age
Shape: Cylinder
Weight: 3 kg
Fat: 50%

Maroilles

Created in AD 962 by a monk in the monastery of Maroilles, this strong-smelling French soft cheese was appreciated by Louis XVI. Protected by AOC regulations, it is turned and brushed during ripening to promote the bacteria which create its distinctively brick red rind. Sorbais, Mignon and Quart de Maroilles are related cheeses. Eaten as a table cheese in France at the end of a meal with beer.

Appearance: Brick-red rind, pale yellow paste
Milk: Cow's
Taste: Tangy, piquant
Texture: Supple
Shape: Square
Size: 13 cm square, 6 cm deep
Weight: 700 g
Fat: 45%

Mascarpone

This soft Italian 'cheese' is in fact made from heated matured cream. Originally from Lombardy, where it was made only in the autumn and winter months, it is now mass-produced all over the country. In Italy itself it is possible to find farmhouse Mascarpone sold wrapped in muslin, but the export version is packed in tubs. It is delicious used in desserts, of which the most famous is tiramisù, layers of coffee- and liqueur-soaked sponge fingers and sweetened Mascarpone. It can also be used in savoury dishes, such as pasta sauces, or in canapé spreads, flavoured with tuna, olives or Gorgonzola.

Appearance: Soft white paste
Milk: Cow's
Taste: Creamy
Texture: Soft, melting
Shape: Sold in tubs
Fat: 90%

Milleens

A farmhouse, semi-soft washed rind cheese from West Cork in Ireland, made by a pioneering Irish cheesemaker influential in the revival of Irish artisanal cheeses. It is made with pasteurised milk from the maker's own herd and two other local herds and traditional rennet. The cheese thrives in the humid conditions which the Cork climate creates naturally. Eat as a table cheese.

Appearance: Orange rind, rich yellow paste
Milk: Cow's
Taste: Full, sweet-sour
Texture: Supple, soft
Shape: Disc
Size: 10 cm diameter, 2.5 cm high; 23 cm diameter, 4 cm high
Weight: 225 g and 1.5 kg
Fat: 45%

Mimolette Français

(Boule de Lille)

Originally ripened in the city of Lille, this French pressed cheese is produced in the same way that Dutch Edam is. The cheese is sold at different ages: Mimolette (three months), *demi-vieille* (six months), *vieille en etuvée* (old), and *très vieille* (very old). It can be eaten at the end of a meal but also used in cooking.

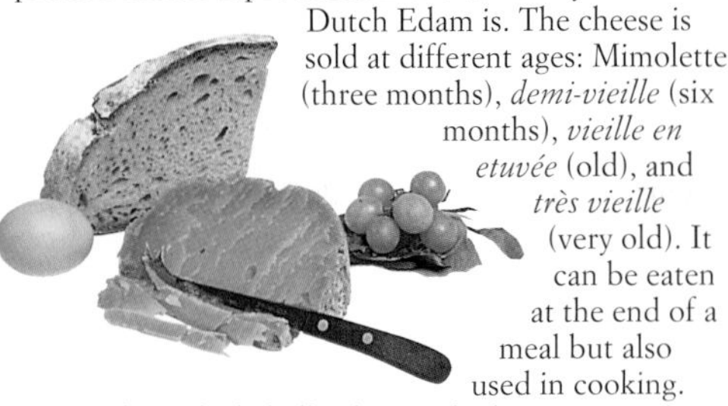

Scooped into little balls, then soaked in port or Madeira for a week, it is served as canapés. The dry cheese can be used as a grating cheese.

Appearance: Orange to grey-brown rind, orange to orange-brown paste
Milk: Cow's
Taste: Nutty to piquant, depending on age

Texture: Semi-hard to hard, depending on age
Shape: Slightly flattened sphere
Size: 20 cm diameter, 15 cm high
Weight: 2-4 kg
Fat: 40%

Monsieur Fromage

A soft factory-made cheese from Normandy, France, enriched with cream. It was invented in the 13th century by Monsieur Fromage (his real name!), after whom it is named.

Appearance: White mould rind, cream-coloured paste
Milk: Cow's
Taste: Mild
Texture: Soft

Shape: Cylinder
Size: 8 cm diameter, 5 cm high
Weight: 250 g
Fat: 60%

Montrachet

A soft French cheese from Burgundy, eaten as a table cheese. The drained curd is ripened in chestnut or vine leaves and sold in its leaf-wrapping.

Appearance: Distinctive chestnut or vine leaf wrapping, white paste
Milk: Goat's
Taste: Mild, creamy
Texture: Supple

Shape: Cylinder
Size: 5-6 cm diameter, 10 cm high
Weight: 75 g
Fat: 45%

Morbier

A French semi-hard pressed cheese, originally created by the cheesemakers of Comte. The distinctive horizontal black streak was created by sprinkling a layer of soot over the curd from an evening's milking to keep away insects, then topping it with the next morning milking's curds. Nowadays food colouring creates the streak. Eaten as a table cheese.

Appearance: Grey or slightly orange crust with a black streak running horizontally through pale yellow paste
Milk: Cow's
Taste: Sweet
Texture: Firm, slightly supple
Shape: Thick disc
Size: 30-40 cm diameter, 6-8 cm high
Weight: 5-9 kg
Fat: 45%

Mozzarella

This well-known Italian cheese, originally made from buffalo's milk, is now made around the world and in many cases has become a pale shadow of the original. True mozzarella's distinctive elastic texture and the way in which it breaks into threads when cooked is due to the way it is produced. Curds are heated until they form an elastic thread which is then wound round into a ball from which small pieces are cut off to make the cheese. It is from this process that mozzarella acquires its name, as *mozzare* means 'to cut off' in Italian. Mozzarella is stored in whey to keep it fresh.

Mozzarella de Bufala, made in Southern Italy from water buffalo's milk mixed with cow's, is the most highly prized, with a softer texture and tangier flavour. Italian delis often stock tiny mozzarellas called *bocconcini* (meaning 'mouthfuls'), marinated in an olive oil dressing and served as antipasti. Lightly smoked mozzarella (*mozzarella affumicata*) is also

available, while strongly smoked mozzarella is called *scamorza*.

In Italy mozzarella is eaten in many forms: simply fresh, dressed with olive oil, with tomato and olives or in a deep-fried sandwich called *mozzarella in carrozza*. Its best-known use in cooking is as a pizza topping.

Appearance: Bright white paste
Milk: Buffalo's or cow's
Taste: Fresh and mild to slightly tangy
Texture: Supple, rubbery
Shape: Slightly flattened ball or block
Fat: 45%

Munster

(Munster Gerome)

An ancient, strong-smelling French soft cheese, first made in monasteries in the 7th century. Its name is derived from *monastère*, French for 'monastery'. AOC regulations stipulate that it is made in certain districts within the Alsace and both factory and farmhouse versions are made. Munster fermier (the farmhouse version) is made in summer in the Vosges mountains and in winter in valley farms. Munster laitier is made all year round from pasteurised milk. Sometimes cumin seeds are added to the cheese, or eaten with it.

Appearance: Light orange bloomy rind, white paste
Milk: Cow's
Taste: Spicy
Texture: Supple
Shape: Flat disc
Size: 7-12 cm diameter, 2-6 cm high; 13-19 cm diameter, 2.4-8 cm high
Weight: 120 g or 450 g
Fat: 45%

Neufchatel

A well-known soft French cheese from the Pays de Bray, Normandy, which dates back to the Middle Ages. Today it is made according to AOC regulations in a variety of shapes, ranging from hearts to squares. The farm-produced version is made in the summer and autumn, while commercially produced cheeses are made all year round. It is sold either fresh, when it is very mild, or ripened (*affine*), when it has a stronger flavour. The white mouldy crust gives a distinct mouldy smell and it is traditionally eaten with bread.

Appearance: White bloomy crust tinged with red if ripened, cream to pale yellow paste
Milk: Cow's
Taste: Fresh and milky to tangy and salty, depending on age
Texture: Smooth, velvety
Shape: Heart, brick, roll, square
Size: Varies
Weight: 100-200 g
Fat: 45%

Ossau-Iraty-Brebis Pyrenées

A French semi-soft cheese from the Bearn and Basque provinces. Made to AOC regulations in small mountain chalets, these Pyrenéan sheep's milk cheeses are ripened for 60 days for the small version and at least 90 days for the larger. The young cheese is eaten as a table cheese while the older, drier cheese is used for grating.

Appearance: Orange-yellow to brown-grey rind, yellow paste dotted with small holes
Milk: Sheep's
Taste: Delicate to mellow, depending on age
Texture: Supple
Shape: Wheel
Size: Varies
Weight: 2-7 kg
Fat: 50%

Paneer

An Indian cheese. Traditionally this was made fresh at home by curdling milk and then straining the curds through cheesecloth and pressing it. Nowadays it is also mass-produced and in countries other than India. The name means simply 'cheese' in most North Indian languages but is now associated with this particular cheese. In Indian cookery it is cut into small cubes, sautéed and used in braised sauce dishes, classically with peas in a North Indian dish called *matar paneer* and also with spinach (*saag paneer*). It can also be crumbled and mixed with grated vegetables such as courgettes to form round rissoles.

Appearance: White paste
Milk: Cow's
Taste: Mild
Texture: Crumbly if home-made, supple if factory-made
Shape: Block
Weight: Varies

Parmesan

This most famous of Italian cheeses, Parmigiano Reggiano is produced in the regions of Parma, Reggio Emilia, Modena, Bologna and Mantova, where it has been made for centuries. It continues to be produced on a small scale in a traditional way in small cheese factories which produce only four to six cheeses a day. Between 1 April and 11 November, unpasteurised cow's milk is used to make huge round cheeses. These great cheeses are then aged for different periods: less than one year for *parmigiano nuovo*; one and a half to two years for *parmigiano vecchio*, and two years or over for a *parmigiano stravecchio*. True Parmesan cheese is stamped with a stencilled 'Parmigiano Reggiano' on its brown rind to mark its authenticity. Characterised as a *grana* or grating cheese, Parmesan is distinguished by its grained, crumbly texture and rich, mellow flavour.

Parmesan enjoys a special place at the heart of Italian cooking. Its most common use is sprinkled grated over pasta dishes, risottos or minestrone, to which it adds a distinctive salty richness of flavour. It is also an essential ingredient of pesto, alongside fresh basil, pine nuts, olive oil and salt, and used to flavour tortellini fillings. In modern British cookery Parmesan shavings rather than gratings are very much in vogue, used to garnish dishes such as roasted vegetables. Good quality Parmesan can also be enjoyed in its own right; a classic combination is alongside ripe pears.

To enjoy Parmesan at its best, avoid pre-grated Parmesan, especially the dried version. Instead, invest in a chunk of fresh Parmesan and grate it as required. When it comes to choosing Parmesan, look for a light golden-coloured cheese, not white-coloured.

Appearance: Hard brown rind, light golden-coloured
Milk: Cow's
Taste: Rich, fruity, mellow
Texture: Grained, crumbly
Shape: Thick cylindrical wheels
Size: 36-46 cm diameter, 18-24 cm tall
Weight: 30-35 kg
Fat: 32%

Pecorino Romano

The most famous of Italy's sheep cheeses (known as pecorino from the Italian *pecore,* meaning 'sheep'), this hard-pressed cheese is made in Lazio according to strict legal criteria laid down in the 1950s. Matured for at least eight months, it is the hardest of Italy's pecorini. It grates well and is used in many robust Roman dishes, sometimes combined with Parmesan.

Other well-known Pecorino cheeses are: Pepato (flavoured with black peppercorns), Sardo (from Sardinia) and Toscano (from Tuscany). Fresh young pecorino is soft with a slight sour tang. In Tuscany and Lazio it is served with the first of the season's young broad beans. Matured pecorino has a sharper flavour.

Appearance: Dark brown, grey or black rind, white-grey paste
Milk: Sheep's
Taste: Tangy, sharp
Texture: Dense
Shape: Cylinder
Size: Varies
Weight: 6-22 kg
Fat: 36%

Perroche

A soft cheese made by hand at Neal's Yard Dairy in Herefordshire, with a noticeably delicate texture. It is sold either plain or decorated and flavoured with fresh dill, tarragon or rosemary. Eat as a table cheese.

Appearance: Small white round cheeses, sold plain or decorated with herbs
Milk: Goat's
Taste: Fresh, slight tang
Texture: Fine-textured, light
Shape: Slightly tapering cylinder
Size: 6 cm diameter base, 5 cm diameter top, 7 cm high
Weight: 150 g
Fat: 45%

Petit Suisse

A dainty soft, fresh French cheese with an extremely light, just-set texture. It was invented in Normandy during the 19th century by Charles Gervais, an ex-patriot Swiss worker – hence the name 'little Swiss'. Its popularity within France means that today it is widely manufactured. Its versatility in the kitchen is one of the reasons for its success. It can be served for dessert with sugar, honey, jam or fruit compote or eaten as a savoury snack, flavoured with fresh herbs, salt and pepper.

Appearance: Bright white paste
Milk: Cow's
Taste: Fresh, slight tang
Texture: Soft
Shape: Cylinder
Size: 3 cm diameter, 4 cm high
Weight: 30 g
Fat: 40%

Pont-l'Évêque

A washed rind Normandy cheese which is thought to be the region's oldest cheese still being made. By the 17th century cheeses from the village of Pont-l'Évêque were sent all over France, such was their popularity. Three litres of milk are needed to make one Pont-l'Évêque, which is protected by AOC regulations. Traditionally, one batch of cheeses was made from the morning milk and one from the evening milk. The rind should not be sticky, hard or greyish, while the interior paste should be soft but not runny. In France it is served at the end of a meal with a full-bodied red wine or cider.

Appearance: Bloomy white-golden rind, white paste
Milk: Cow's
Taste: Tangy
Texture: Soft, supple
Shape: Square block
Size: 10.5-11 cm square, 3 cm high
Weight: 350-400 g
Fat: 45%

Port-Salut

An industrially produced, pressed French cheese made from pasteurised milk. The name comes from a French monastery at Entrammes where a cheese called Port-Salut was originally created. In the 1950s, however, the monks sold the trademark name to a commercial creamery, continuing to make their own cheese but calling it either Entrammes or Port-du-Salut. A mild cheese, the commercial version is served as a dessert cheese or used to make croque-monsieur (a snack of ham and melted cheese served on toast).

Appearance: A light orange rind, cream-coloured paste
Milk: Cow's
Taste: Light
Texture: Supple
Shape: Wheel
Size: 20 cm diameter, 4 cm high
Weight: 1.3-1.5 kg
Fat: 50%

Provolone

An Italian curd cheese which comes originally from the south of Italy, with the best coming from Campania and Apulia. It is now also produced in the Po Valley in Northern Italy. The kneaded curd is made into a variety of shapes, ranging from small ovals to large pear shapes. *Provolette* is the name for the small cheeses, *provole* the medium-sized and *provoloni* the large. Young provolone is sweet and softer than the mature *provolone piccante*, aged for up to two years. Eaten as a table cheese.

Appearance: Creamy white to deep yellow paste, depending on age
Milk: Cow's
Taste: From mild to piquant
Texture: Supple
Shape: Various
Size: Various
Weight: 200 g to 30 kg
Fat: 44%

Quark

Originally a German cheese (the name means 'curds' in German), this fresh unripened curd cheese is now widely produced. The fat content varies according to the type of milk used: skimmed, whole or buttermilk, plus cream. A versatile cheese, this can be served with fruit or used in dips, while in cooking it is used in cheesecakes and baked flans.

Appearance: Soft white paste
Milk: Cow's
Taste: Mild, slightly sour
Texture: Soft
Fat: 10-60%

Raclette

One of a group of semi-hard Swiss cheeses from the Valais canton. Its name means 'scraping', a meaning that becomes clear when one discovers that it is used in a traditional Swiss dish also called raclette. To make the dish a whole cheese is halved. The cut surface is then heated before an open fire and the melted cheese scraped onto a plate to be eaten at once with boiled potatoes, pickled onions and gherkins. The scraped rind, coated with melted cheese, is called a *religieuse* and is much-coveted. It is also eaten as a dessert cheese.

Appearance: A grey-brown rind with a golden paste pocked with a few holes
Milk: Cow's

Taste: Fruity
Texture: Supple
Shape: Cylinder
Weight: 5-7 kg
Fat: 50%

Ragstone

A farmhouse semi-soft cheese, made by the Neal's Yard Creamery in Herefordshire. The creamery was originally based at the Ragstone Ridge in Kent, hence the cheese's name. Matured for two to three weeks, it can be eaten on its own or grilled.

Appearance: White bloomy rind, white paste
Milk: Goat's
Taste: Fresh, slight tang
Texture: Light, smooth
Shape: Log
Size: 15-16 cm long, 5 cm diameter
Fat: 45%

Rauchkäse

The generic German term for smoked cheese. The majority of 'Bavarian smoked cheese' is mass-made processed cheese, made by blending together cheeses such as Gouda and Emmentaler and adding artificial smoky flavourings.

Reblochon

An ancient French soft cheese from the Savoie, noted for its freshness and mildness. The name comes from the French verb *reblocher*, meaning 'to milk a second time'. The story goes that the herdsmen would purposely not milk their cows dry. Once the farmer had checked the yield the rich milk was used by the herdsmen to make cheese for their own consumption. The cheese is still produced in the Savoie according to AOC regulations, made from the thick milk of the second milking in farmhouses, farmers' co-operatives or factories. It is made in two sizes: regular and a smaller version called the Petit Reblochon. It is eaten as a dessert cheese.

Appearance: Yellow, pink or orange rind with white bloom, ivory paste
Milk: Cow's
Taste: Delicate, creamy with slight nuttiness

Texture: Very supple
Shape: Flattened disc
Size: 9-14 cm diameter, 3-3.5 cm high
Weight: 240-550 g
Fat: 45%

Ribblesdale Superior Goat

A farmhouse hard, pressed cheese, made in Horton-in-Ribblesdale in Yorkshire from pasteurised milk and non-GM vegetarian rennet. The cheese is wax-coated and matured for four to six weeks. There is also a smoked version. Eat as a table cheese or use in salads.

Appearance: Primrose yellow or green wax coating, white paste
Milk: Goat's
Taste: Fresh, piquant
Texture: Supple
Shape: Wheel
Weight: 2 kg
Fat: 56%

Ricotta

An Italian whey cheese, made by heating the leftover whey once the heated curds have been removed. The name literally means 're-cooked'. Authentic ricotta is made from sheep's milk, but the mass-produced ricotta for export is made from cow's milk. Nowadays, too, whole or skimmed milk is often used to enrich it. Traditionally, ricotta was drained in rush baskets, giving it a characteristic shape and basketwork markings.

Its inoffensive blandness make it a very versatile cheese in the kitchen. It is widely used in Italian cooking and has an especial affinity with spinach. Its savoury uses include spinach and ricotta gnocchi (dumplings), stuffed pancakes, vegetable pies and as a filling for tortellini and cannelloni. Sweet dishes include *cannoli* (deep-fried pastry tubes filled with sweetened ricotta), cheesecakes, tarts and *ricotta al caffè* (mixed with sugar, ground coffee and rum).

Drained, salted, sun-dried ricotta (called *salata* or *stagionata*) can be found in Italian delis. This originates from Southern Italy where it is grated onto pasta, with tomato sauce adding a salty savouriness.

Appearance: White paste
Milk: Cow's or sheep's

Taste: Delicate, fresh
Texture: Soft, smooth
Fat: Varies

Roquefort

This is France's best-known blue cheese, famously ripened in caves in Aquitane. An ancient cheese, it dates back at least to Roman times when it was mentioned by Pliny the Elder. It was the Emperor Charlemagne's favourite cheese, while Casanova attributed it with aphrodisiac qualities. In 1411 Charles VI granted the people of Roquefort the monopoly for ripening the cheeses in their caves as it had been done for centuries before. Today's Roquefort production is protected by AOC regulations, the first of their kind, passed in 1925. The cheese is cured at Roquefort-sur-Soulzon and must be ripened for at least three months in the dark, cold natural caves of the commune. The blue mould found only in these

caves is called *Penicillium roqueforti* and it is this mould which is used to create the blue cheese. Fresh young cheeses are pierced with needles and exposed to spore-laden air. As the cheese ripens it develops its distinctive patterning of mould, which varies according to age. It is sold foil-wrapped, often in slices, but ideally to savour it at its best one should buy a piece freshly taken from a whole cheese.

Classically it is eaten as an after-dinner cheese, accompanied by a sweet wine such as a Sauternes or a full-bodied red such as Chateauneuf-du-Pape. It is also used in a number of recipes: to make canapés, flavoured butters to serve with grilled meat, sauces or in Pears Savarin (Roquefort-stuffed pears).

Appearance: White to cream paste, mottled with green-blue veins
Milk: Sheep's
Taste: Rich, spicy
Texture: Moist, crumbly
Shape: Tall cylinder
Size: 19-20 cm diameter, 8.5-10.5 cm high
Weight: 2.5-2.9 kg
Fat: 52%

Saint-Marcellin

(Tomme de Saint-Marcellin)

Originally this small, unpressed French cheese was made from goat's milk, but today it is largely made from cow's milk. Its most famous admirer was King Louis XI, who came across it while he was a prince and ordered that it should be served at the royal palaces. It is eaten as a dessert cheese, accompanied by soft, fruity red wines.

Appearance: Thin bloomy rind, varying in colour from pale to dark golden yellow
Milk: Cow's or goat's
Taste: Mild with a tang
Texture: Soft
Shape: Flat disc
Size: 7 cm diameter, 2-2.5 cm high
Weight: 80 g
Fat: 40%

Saint-Nectaire

A distinctive musty-smelling, semi-hard French cheese from the Auvergne. Enjoyed by Louis XIV, it is made according to AOC regulations in farmhouses, co-operative dairies and factories. Cheeses made with unpasteurised milk have a more complex flavour than those made with pasteurised. As the cheese ripens it develops its characteristic smell and flavour. Farmhouse (*fermier*) cheeses have an oval plaque on the rind, while factory versions have a rectangular one. Eaten as a table cheese.

Appearance: Grey-brown rind patched with orange mould, golden paste
Milk: Cow's
Taste: Earthy
Texture: Supple

Shape: Flat disc
Size: 13 cm or 21 cm diameter, 3.5 cm or 5 cm high
Weight: 600 g or 1.7 kg
Fat: 45%

Saint-Paulin

A French pressed cheese modelled upon the monastery cheeses, especially Port-Salut. First made around 1930, it is now made from pasteurised milk throughout France. There is also a version made from unpasteurised milk. Ripened for two to three weeks, the orange-coloured rind shows traces of the cloth in which the cheese was wrapped when pressed. It can be served as a dessert cheese but is also used in croque-monsieur and mixed salads.

Appearance: Orange rind, ivory paste
Milk: Cow's
Taste: Mild, sweet
Texture: Smooth
Shape: Thick disc
Size: 8-13 cm diameter, 3-4.5 cm high or 20 cm diameter, 4-6 cm high
Weight: 500 g-1.5 kg or 1.8-2 kg
Fat: 40%

Salers

A traditional hard pressed cheese from the Auvergne in France. This is the *fermier* (farmhouse or mountain chalet) version of Cantal, made according to AOC regulations. These stipulate that Salers can only be made with milk from cattle grazed on mountain pastures in the summer between 1 May and 30 October. During production it is pressed twice, giving it a characteristic firm texture and a rich depth of flavour. It is ripened for a minimum of three months but sometimes for as long as 18 months. Eaten as a table cheese.

Appearance: Thick brown-coloured rind with yellow paste
Milk: Cow's
Taste: Full, mellow, nutty
Texture: Firm
Shape: Cylinder
Size: 38-48 cm diameter, 30-40 cm high
Weight: 30-40 kg
Fat: 45%

Savaron

A pressed cheese from the Auvergne, similar to Saint-Nectaire and Saint-Paulin. Made commercially from pasteurised milk, it is a washed rind cheese, ripened in humid cellars which gives it a strong smell of mould. It is usually eaten as a dessert cheese.

Appearance: Grey rind with golden paste
Milk: Cow's
Taste: Mild
Texture: Supple
Shape: Thick disc
Size: 20 cm diameter, 4-6.5 cm high
Weight: 1.5 kg
Fat: 45%

Selles-sur-Cher

(Romorantin)

A delicately-flavoured French goat's cheese from Berry. Made to AOC regulations, this is a dry-cured cheese with a natural rind coated with powdered charcoal which gives it its dark coat. Eat as a dessert cheese.

Appearance: Wrinkled rind, dusted with dark ash, bright white paste
Milk: Goat's
Taste: Mild, nutty
Texture: Smooth, fine-textured
Shape: Tapering cylinder
Size: 8 cm diameter at base, 7 cm diameter at top, 2.3 cm high
Weight: 150-200 g
Fat: 45%

Serra

The best-known of Portugal's cheeses, historically this comes from the Serra da Estrela in the Beira region. It is an ancient cheese, traditionally made on the farms but now also imitated commercially. When young (four to six weeks) it is soft and buttery, but when aged for a further five months it hardens and develops a fuller, more pronounced flavour, whereupon it is sold as Serra Velho. Tipo Serra is the inferior, harder factory-made version. In Portugal the aged version is commonly served with *marmelada* (quince paste).

Appearance:Golden rind with pale buttery yellow paste dotted with small holes
Milk: Sheep's
Taste: Fresh
Texture: Creamy and buttery to supple, depending on age
Shape: Cylinder
Size: 18 cm diameter
Weight: 1.5-2 kg
Fat: 45%

Sharpham

A farmhouse unpressed mould rind soft cheese made at Sharpham House, Ashprington in Devon. The unpasteurised milk comes from the estate's own herd of Jersey cattle and gives a distinctive creaminess to this Couloummiers-style cheese. The maker uses non-GM rennet and there are plans to convert the cheese to organic. Eat as a table cheese.

Appearance: White bloomy rind, yellow paste
Milk: Cow's
Taste: Creamy with a grassy tang
Texture: Supple-soft
Shape: Square or disc
Size: 10 cm square, 2.5 cm high; 20 cm diameter, 2.5 cm high
Weight: 250 g or 1 kg
Fat: 45%

Shropshire Blue

An English semi-hard blue-veined cheese which, despite its name, is actually made in Nottinghamshire. The distinctive orange-coloured paste is achieved by adding Annatto (a natural vegetable dye). Eat as a table cheese.

Appearance: Brown speckled rind with a rich orange-coloured interior with blue veining
Milk: Cow's

Taste: Mildly savoury
Texture: Firm
Shape: Cylinder
Size: Varies
Weight: Varies
Fat: 34%

Single Gloucester

A traditional English cheese, now very rare and made only on a handful of farms in Gloucestershire. Now under a Protected Designation of Origin order, Single Gloucester must be made in Gloucestershire alone. One maker produces it from the milk of his herd of Old Gloucester cattle.

The cheese is historically related to Double Gloucester. It differed in that it was traditionally made partly from skimmed milk and not coloured as Double Gloucester is. It is matured for only three to 12 weeks. Eat as a table cheese or use as a grilling cheese.

Appearance: White paste
Milk: Cow's
Taste: Sweet-sharp
Texture: Firm
Shape: Millstones or truckles
Size: Varies
Weight: 900 g to 3.5 kg

Spenwood

A farmhouse hard cheese made in Berkshire, with the firm translucent paste characteristic of hard sheep's milk cheeses. It can either be eaten as a dessert cheese or used as a grilling or grating cheese.

Appearance: Grey hard rind, pale yellow paste
Milk: Sheep's
Taste: Sweet and mild when young, stronger and nuttier when mature
Texture: Dense, drier when mature
Shape: Wheel
Weight: 2 kg
Fat: 50%

Stilton

One of the world's great blue cheeses, Stilton is considered the 'king of English cheeses'. The only British cheese to be protected by legal regulations along the lines of the French Appellation d'Origine Controllée (AOC) scheme, it is produced by traditional methods by 12 dairies in Leicestershire, Nottinghamshire and Derbyshire. It is an ancient cheese, dating back to at least the turn of the 18th century. It was thought to originate in the area around Melton Mowbray, but gained its name and its fame in the town of Stilton, where it was sold at the Bell Inn to coach travellers on the Great North Road. In 1727 the author Daniel Defoe wrote of the town of Stilton as being 'famous for cheese, which is called our English Parmesan, and is brought to the table with the mites or maggots around, so thick, that they bring a spoon with them for you to eat the mites with, as you do the cheese.'

To encourage the characteristic moulding, a culture

of *Penicillium roqueforti* is added to the milk and the cheeses are pierced to encourage veining. The cheeses are ripened for between three to four months and as they age the mould spreads and the flavour develops. In addition to Blue Stilton, White Stilton is also produced, although on a much smaller scale. This is eaten much younger and has a sharper flavour. Although Blue Stilton is available throughout the year, it is supposed to be at its best in the autumn when it has been made with the rich summer milk. When choosing Stilton look for even veining and a clear contrast between the paste and the veins.

Stilton is traditionally served as a dessert cheese accompanied by port and is especially popular at Christmas time. The best way to cut a whole Stilton or a truckle is across the top, forming a 'lid'. When servings have been evenly cut from the open surface seal the surface with clingfilm and top with the lid.

Appearance: Grey rind, densely blue-veined ivory paste
Milk: Cow's
Taste: Spicy, mellow

Texture: Firm to creamy, depending on age
Shape: Tall cylinder
Size: Varies
Weight: 2-8 kg
Fat: 48%

Stinking Bishop

As the characterful name suggests, this is a potent-smelling English semi-soft washed rind cheese, made by one maker in Gloucestershire. It is made from pasteurised milk and a non-GM vegetarian rennet. The rind is washed with perry, an alcoholic drink made with pears which was traditionally produced in Gloucestershire. Stinking Bishop is, in fact, the name of a local pear variety used in perry. The inspiration for the cheese was the French Trappist cheeses made by Cistercian monks. Eaten as a table cheese, this goes well with perry or Gewürztraminer wine.

Appearance: An orange-yellow rind, rich yellow paste
Milk: Cow's
Taste: Full, meaty
Texture: Creamy-supple
Shape: Wheel
Weight: 1.5-1.8 kg
Fat: 48%

Sussex Slipcote

A recently produced English soft cheese made, however, to a recipe dating back to the 16th century. There is a venerable tradition of slipcote cheeses in Britain. Traditionally this was a rich, creamy cheese, usually wrapped in leaves or reeds, while the name is thought to refer to the way in which the cheeses 'slipped' off their 'coats' as they became soft and runny. Eaten as a table cheese.

Appearance: Pale, nearly white paste
Milk: Sheep's
Taste: Light, creamy with a delicate tang, also flavoured with garlic and herbs or peppercorns
Texture: Soft
Shape: Buttons or logs
Size: 5 cm diameter, 2 cm deep or 18 cm long, 6 cm deep
Weight: 100 g and 1 kg
Fat: 45%

Swaledale

An English semi-hard pressed cheese, made using traditional methods in the north of England. Historically, this type of cheese dates back to the Middle Ages when it was made by the prosperous monasteries of the Dales. The cow's milk cheeses are also smoked or flavoured with chives and garlic, applemint or soaked in Old Peculier ale. Eaten as a table cheese.

Appearance: Dark yellow rind, pale cream paste
Milk: Cow's or goat's or sheep's
Taste: Fresh
Texture: Moist
Shape: Truckles
Size: Varies
Weight: 250 g to 3 kg
Fat: 48%

Taleggio

A rich semi-soft, unpressed cheese, traditionally from Lombardy in Italy. Generally, Taleggio is eaten at around 40 days old. Mature Taleggio, ripened for around 80 days, takes on a more aromatic flavour and a darker colour. It is eaten as a dessert cheese.

Appearance: Pink-red crust, pale yellow paste
Milk: Cow's
Taste: Mild, fruity
Texture: Supple, tender
Shape: Square
Size: 20 cm square
Weight: 2 kg
Fat: 48% min

Teifi

A Welsh farmhouse hard cheese, often compared to Gouda. It is made from unpasteurised cheese using vegetarian rennet. It is also available smoked or flavoured with cumin. Eat as a dessert cheese or use as a grating and grilling cheese.

Appearance: Smooth orange rind, yellow paste
Milk: Cow's
Taste: Fruity when young, spicy fullness when mature
Texture: Dense
Shape: Millstone
Size: Varies
Weight: 450 g, 900 g and 3.5 kg

Tête-de-Moine

(Bellelay)

A Swiss cheese first created in the monastery of Bellelay, although it is now made in dairies. This is a seasonal cheese, available in the autumn and winter. Traditionally it goes on sale when the first leaves of autumn begin to fall. The name, which means 'monk's head', is reputed to come from the old custom at the monastery of Bellelay of giving the prior one cheese for each monk. Alternatively, some say it refers to the appearance of the cheese when it was traditionally served with the top cut off and a strip of rind trimmed off all the way round. It is eaten as a dessert cheese, when thin slivers are shaved from the surface, and in Switzerland it is seasoned with ground pepper and cumin.

Appearance: Yellowish rind, golden-yellow paste
Milk: Cow's
Taste: Spicy, fruity

Texture: Firm, slightly supple
Shape: Cylinder
Size: Varies
Weight: 500 g to 2 kg
Fat: 50%

Ticklemore

A farmhouse hard cheese, with a distinctive shape and ridged rind from the mould in which it is drained. It is made from unpasteurised milk and non-GM vegetarian rennet. Eat as a table cheese.

Appearance: Knobbly brown-grey rind, white paste
Milk: Goat's
Taste: Subtle, slight tang
Texture: Dense
Shape: Basket
Weight: 1.8 kg

Tilsit

A semi-hard German cheese originally made in the 19th century and named after the town of Tilsit. The skimmed milk variety is sometimes flavoured with caraway seeds. Traditionally the cheese was made in wheel shapes, but with factory production it is increasingly made in blocks. Eaten as a table cheese or used as a grilling cheese.

Appearance: Dark yellow rind, yellow paste dotted with tiny holes
Milk: Cow's
Taste: Delicate
Texture: Supple
Shape: Wheel or block
Size: Varies
Weight: Varies
Fat: 30-50%

Tomme de Savoie

A generic term given to a whole variety of pressed semi-hard French cheeses made in the Savoie region. The word *tomme* (or *tome*) is used to describe small French farmhouse cheeses. Nowadays, Tomme de Savoie are produced in farmhouses, co-operative dairies or in factories and ripened for at least four weeks.

A distinct smell of mould is one of their characteristics, but the flavour is mild. Variants include Tomme au Marc, fermented in marc brandy, and Tomme de Savoie au Cumin, flavoured with cumin seeds. They are eaten as table cheeses, dessert cheeses or used in sandwiches.

Appearance: Hard grey rind, patched with red and yellow, ivory to pale yellow paste pocked with a few holes of various sizes
Milk: Cow's
Taste: Slight nuttiness
Texture: Supple with a slight stickiness
Shape: Flat cylinder
Size: 18-30 cm diameter, 5-8 cm high
Weight: 1.5-3 kg
Fat: 20-40%

Tymsboro'

A farmhouse soft cheese, made on a farm at Timsbury in Somerset with unpasteurised milk from the maker's own flock and natural rennet. The natural rind is coated with black ash and then develops a white mould layer. It is matured for between two to four weeks and eaten as a dessert cheese.

Appearance: A grey-black rind, white paste
Milk: Goat's
Taste: Fresh, tangy
Texture: Smooth, fine-textured

Shape: Truncated pyramid
Weight: 250 g

Tyning

An English farmhouse hard cheese, reminiscent of Italian Pecorino. It is made from unpasteurised milk from the maker's own herd of sheep and traditional rennet. Eat as a table cheese. Mature Tyning can also be grated and is delicious over pasta.

Appearance: Brown-grey rind, light yellow paste
Milk: Sheep's
Taste: Nutty, fruity
Texture: Hard
Shape: Basket
Size: 23 cm diameter, 9 cm high
Weight: 2.25-3.25 kg
Fat: 45%

Vacherin Mont d'Or

A renowned soft Swiss cheese made from unpasteurised milk in mountain chalets and sold wrapped with a strip of pine bark around it. When ripe the crust is removed and the soft paste inside spooned out. In Switzerland it is served sprinkled with cumin seeds and accompanied by boiled potatoes or as a dessert cheese. If buying a whole Vacherin make sure you do not buy one too large, as once cut the cheese should be eaten as soon as possible. There is also a very similar French cheese of the same name, made in the Franche-Comte.

Appearance: Smooth pink rind, dull yellow paste
Milk: Cow's
Taste: Mild, faint hint of pine
Texture: Soft, smooth
Shape: Cylinder
Size: Varies
Weight: 200 g to 3 kg
Fat: 50%

Valençay

(Pyramide)

The farmhouse (*fermier*) version of this French soft cheese is made in the province of Berry and is available from spring through to autumn. The charcoal-dusted rind and distinctive flattened pyramid shape make it easy to spot. Valençay Laitier is the commercial version, made all year round from frozen goat's milk. It has a white bloomy rind and a stronger goaty smell and flavour than the farmhouse one. It is served as a dessert cheese.

Appearance: Smooth white paste
Milk: Goat's
Taste: Delicate to strong, depending on method of production
Texture: Firm
Shape: Flattened pyramid
Size: Varies
Weight: 45 g to 250 g
Fat: 45%

Vulscombe

A soft-pressed English farmhouse cheese made in Devon. The makers use the acid curd method, employed by agricultural workers in the 18th and 19th centuries, where the curd coagulates without the aid of rennet. The cheese is eaten when young at one to three weeks old and is characterised by its fresh, clean flavour. Added flavourings include herbs and garlic or crushed black peppercorns. Eat as a table cheese.

Appearance: White paste
Milk: Goat's
Taste: Mild
Texture: Creamy

Shape: Small rounded cylinder
Size: 6 cm diameter, 4 cm deep
Weight: 180 g
Fat: 45%

Waterloo

A semi-soft farmhouse English cheese, made in Berkshire from thermised Guernsey cows' milk which gives it its characteristic rich colour. The maker uses the Coulommiers method in which undrained curds are placed in moulds and the only pressure comes by stacking the moulds. It matures in four to 10 weeks and is eaten as a table cheese.

Appearance: Whitish brown rind, bright yellow paste
Milk: Cow's
Taste: Creamy, grassy
Texture: Soft and moist
Shape: Cylinder
Weight: 400 g and 1.5 kg
Fat: 45%

Wealden Round

A recently created soft English cheese eaten fresh and young. Made by Neal's Yard Creamery, there are plans to make it from organic milk. Flavourings include parsley and garlic, chive, tarragon, spring onion, black pepper and garlic. Eaten as a table cheese with crackers or bread.

Appearance: Ivory paste dotted with herbs or pepper
Milk: Cow's
Taste: Mild
Texture: Soft, just-set
Shape: Disc
Size: 10 cm diameter, 3 cm high
Weight: 200 g

Wensleydale

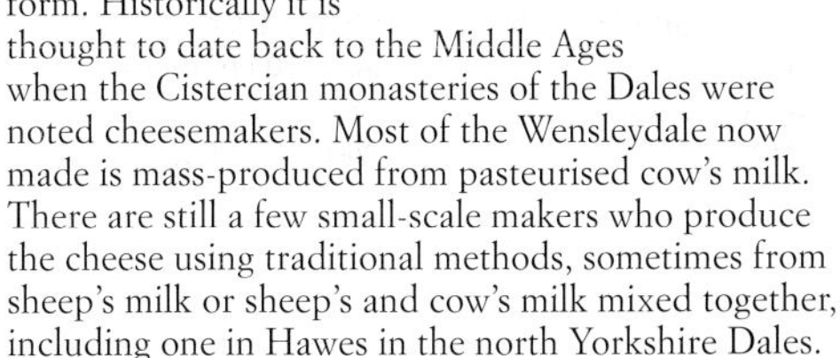

This ancient English cheese was originally known as a blue-veined cheese, but is now widely sold in its white unveined form. Historically it is thought to date back to the Middle Ages when the Cistercian monasteries of the Dales were noted cheesemakers. Most of the Wensleydale now made is mass-produced from pasteurised cow's milk. There are still a few small-scale makers who produce the cheese using traditional methods, sometimes from sheep's milk or sheep's and cow's milk mixed together, including one in Hawes in the north Yorkshire Dales.

Usually it is sold young when it has a mild, fresh flavour. In Yorkshire it is traditionally served with a slice of fruitcake or apple pie.

Appearance: White paste
Milk: Cow's and sheep's
Taste: Light, milky
Texture: Slightly flaky
Shape: Cylinder or block
Size: Varies
Weight: 4-6 kg
Fat: 48%

Wigmore

A semi-soft English farmhouse cheese from Berkshire with a natural mould rind. Eat as a table cheese.

Appearance: Pink-orange to grey rind depending on age, white paste
Milk: Sheep's

Taste: Sweet, slightly nutty
Texture: Soft
Shape: Wheel
Weight: 400 g or 1.5 kg
Fat: 48%

Glossary

Annatto: a natural red food dye used to colour certain cheeses.

Appellation d'Origine Controllée (AOC): French laws which regulate how certain cheeses are produced within a certain region of France following established methods. There are 34 AOC cheeses in France.

Chèvre: the term given to French goat's cheeses.

Chymosin: the name of a genetically modified vegetarian rennet.

Coagulation: the clotting of milk, usually triggered by rennet.

Croque-monsieur: a French hot sandwich which is a popular café dish made from crustless bread filled with thinly sliced Gruyère cheese and lean ham, lightly browned either by frying in butter or grilling.

Curd: coagulated fats and other solids made from milk.

Farmhouse cheese: a term used to describe cheeses made in traditional ways rather than mass-produced. Often farmhouse cheeses are made on a small scale by cheesemakers using milk from their own herds or that of neighbouring farms.

Fat content: expressed as a percentage of fat in dry matter (after all the water has been eliminated).

Paste: the term used to describe the interior of a cheese. The French use the term pâté.

Rauchkäse: the generic German term for smoked cheese.

Rennet: an enzyme derived from calf's stomachs traditionally used to coagulate milk in cheesemaking. The term 'traditional rennet' is used to describe calf's stomach rennet.

Trappist cheese: a generic term for various French cheeses made by monks in Trappist monasteries.

Triple cream: a type of rich soft cheese made by adding cream during the cheesemaking process.

Vegetarian rennet: a coagulating agent not derived from calf's stomachs and, therefore, deemed suitable for vegetarians. Chymosin is a vegetarian rennet created using genetic modification.

Whey: what is left of the milk after the coagulated curd has been removed.

Specialist Cheese Shops

LONDON

Barstow & Barr
32-34 Earls Court Road
London W8
(0207-937 8004)

Cheeses
13 Fortis Green Road
London N10
(0208-444 9141)

La Fromagerie
30 Highbury Park
London N5 2AA
(0207-359 7440)
(mail order)

Hamish Johnston
48 Northcote Road
London SW11
(0207-738 0741)

Neal's Yard Dairy
17 Shorts Gardens
London WC2
(0207-379 7646)

Also at:
Borough Market
6 Park Street,
London SE1
(0207-407 1800)
(mail-order)

Paxton & Whitfield
93 Jermyn Street
London SW1 6JE
(0207-930 0259)
(mail order)

Rippon Cheese Stores
26 Upper Tachbrook St
London SW1V 1SW
(0207-931 0628)
(mail order)

SOUTH-EAST ENGLAND

Teddington Cheese
42 Station Road
Teddington
Middlesex TW11 9AA
(0208-977 6868)
(mail order)

Vivians
2 Worple Way
Richmond
Surrey
TW10 6DF
(0208-940 3600)

SOUTH-WEST ENGLAND

Paxton & Whitfield
1 John Street
Bath BA1 2JL
(01225- 466403)

Ticklemore Cheese Shop
1 Ticklemore Street
Totnes
Devon TQ9 5EJ
(01803-865926)

MIDLANDS

Paxton & Whitfield
13 Wood Street
Stratford-upon-Avon
CV37 6JF
(01789 415544)

NORTH-WEST ENGLAND

The Cheese Shop
116 Northgate Street
Chester
CH1 2HT
(01244-346240)

SCOTLAND

I.J. Mellis Cheesemonger
30a Victoria Street,
Edinburgh EH1 2JW
(0131-226 6215)

also at:
205 Bruntsfield Place
Edinburgh
EH10 4DH
(0131-447 8889)

also at:
492 Great Western Road
Glasgow
(0141-339 8998)
(mail-order)

COLLINS GEM
BABIES' names
a
?
z
a mine of information

COLLINS GEM
BEER
a mine of information

COLLINS GEM
BIRDS
a mine of information

COLLINS GEM
CALORIE
Counter
a mine of information

COLLINS GEM
FACT FILE
a mine of information

COLLINS GEM
FENG SHUI
a mine of information

COLLINS GEM
FLAGS
a mine of information

COLLINS GEM
Healthy
EATING
a mine of information

COLLINS GEM
QUOTATIONS
a mine of information

COLLINS GEM
SAS
Self-Defence
a mine of information

COLLINS GEM
SAS
Survival Guide
a mine of information

COLLINS GEM
SEASHORE
a mine of information

COLLINS GEM
TREES
a mine of information

COLLINS GEM
Understanding
DREAMS
a mine of information

COLLINS GEM
WILD
flowers
a mine of information

COLLINS GEM
WINE
Dictionary
a mine of information